LF

The Rights of Infants

The Rights of Infants

EARLY PSYCHOLOGICAL NEEDS

AND THEIR SATISFACTION

Margaretha Antoinette Ribble

MARGARET A. RIBBLE, M.D.

Second Edition

COLUMBIA UNIVERSITY PRESS
New York and London

Margaret A. Ribble, M.D., is a practicing psychiatrist and psychoanalyst. Dr. Ribble's experience has included pediatrics and general medicine. She is the author of *The Personality of the Young Child.*

Copyright 1943, © 1965 Columbia University Press

Second edition 1965
ISBN 0-231-02849-0

Library of Congress Catalog Card Number: 65-24832
Printed in the United States of America

10 9 8 7 6 5 4 3

To all inquiring parents

Preface to the Second Edition

TWENTY YEARS have elapsed since the first publication of these findings from the study of infants and their parents. During these years in the daily practice of psychiatry and psychoanalysis it has been possible to check the validity of our earlier conclusions. It is unquestionably true that adverse emotional experiences between child and parents in the first two years of life can evoke serious problems in the child's personality development.

In the course of therapy with young parents and others it was often possible to bring into perspective the origin of such problems as constant friction between father and son or mother and daughter often involving open delinquency, or else withdrawal with neurotic tendencies. The readjustment of such deviations in adolescence or later life is a long and tedious process, often successful, sometimes not. The ideal approach would be prevention as far as possible by a better understanding of an infant's essential emotional needs and the processes of his psychological maturing. The suffering in neurotic illness and the waste of energy and loss of creative drive entailed are deplorable.

Little has been added to this new edition except for increased emphasis in two basic areas: 1) the role of the father in the early personal adjustment of the young child to an understanding of maleness and femaleness, which can become a life problem; 2) renewed direction of parents to the recognition of early erotic impulses in the baby without alarm or condemnation so that they may be diverted, when excessive, into appropriate play activities with parents and family.

In the final chapter some life histories are appended which may help to clarify the dynamics of early maturing difficulties and the ways in which they are related to emotional illness in later life.

MARGARET A. RIBBLE

Knoxville, Tennessee
April, 1965

Contents

The Rights of Infants

The Right to a Mother

WHEN SCIENCE and instinct seem to clash, many of us are on both sides of the argument at once. We can understand the dog who tears the bandage from his paw, meekly indicating "I know you meant well, but something tells me this is all wrong; the thing to do is to lick it." We can sympathize even better with the veterinary who put it there for a good reason. If we are curious enough to observe closely a great many examples of this kind, we usually find that both sides of this vital science-instinct argument contain truth. Science, on the one hand, has tested and proven reasons for doing what it does but has failed to take into account some of the deep-hidden forces of instinct. In fact, there is a great need for a meeting ground where a science-of-instinct may develop. Instinct is a powerful form of natural energy, perhaps comparable in humans to electrictity or even atomic energy in the mechanical world. It is a free gift of nature and has to do with the will to live, to grow, and to take an important role in the lives of other human beings. When it is utilized and controlled, it can strengthen and enrich life's finest activities—loving, thinking, and, finally, understanding.

Maternal instinct, which we are considering here, is one

that has suffered considerably in our modern way of life. It is no longer a compelling force in many women; other interests have crowded it out. Breast-feeding, for example, which simplifies immeasurably the infant's first adjustment to life, has, to some extent, gone "out of style."

The purpose of this book is to take up a vital aspect of infant care which is not covered in manuals dealing with food and general hygiene—that is, the feeling life of a baby, the emotional reactions which get their initial momentum and direction in the primary relationship between child and mother. Modern science, when it considers infant needs, assumes that this basic mother-child tie exists in order that the child may be fed and protected from objective harm during his helpless infancy. This theory, if it stops there, makes the function of the mother that of a trustworthy nurse, who can be arbitrarily replaced. It leaves out the matter of personal relationship on which the child's subsequent emotional and social adjustments are based.

This attitude is psychologically inadequate—so much so that the infant who is treated impersonally, however well-nourished and clean he may be, is definitely handicapped in his personality growth and in his early capacity to trust and respond to others. Such an impersonal attitude at the beginning sets the stage for innumerable behavior problems and irregular habits later on—for friction and disappointment between parent and child, for reluctance to cooperate or comply in matters of learning the primary activities of eating, sleeping, and being clean. It may also be responsible for an attitude of withdrawal into exaggerated fantasy.

Since all good science begins by defining its terms, it is essential to make clear what we mean by the earliest mothering. It is, to begin with, a continuance of the closeness of the prenatal state, with the additional factor of touch or contact. The more clearly it imitates certain conditions before birth the more successful it is in the first weeks. The newborn baby still needs to be rocked gently as he was inside his mother's body. He needs to be carried about at regular intervals, until such time as he can move and coordinate his own body. This helps to strengthen his sense of equilibrium and to give him his first feeling of belonging. Also, he needs frequent periods of close contact with his mother, for this warmth and holding gradually takes the place of the physical connection before birth when the child was like an organ of the mother's body. Contact is an important stimulus to sensory growth and awareness. In addition, mothering includes the whole gamut of small acts by which an emotionally healthy mother may consistently show her love for her child, thus instinctively stimulating emotional responses in him. Obviously, feeding, bathing, and all the details of physical care come in, but, in addition to these duties, which can easily become routine and perfunctory, we mean all of the small evidences of tender feeling—fondling, caressing, and singing or speaking to the baby. These activities, when used without excess or intrusion, have a deep significance in eliciting awareness.

A Swiss colleague had defined the complete mother as one who is able to give her baby a sublimated form of devotion, "without hesitation, without feeling of duty, without sensual joy, and without a feeling of sacrifice."

Several decades ago, one of the most baffling problems of child health was a disease known as marasmus. The name comes from a Greek word which means "wasting away." Sometimes it was also called infantile atrophy or debility. It affected particularly children in the first year of life, and at that time it was responsible for more than half the deaths of babies in that age group.

To combat this tragic evil a special study of infant care was undertaken by both medical and social agencies, and the astonishing discovery was made that babies in the best homes and hospitals, given the most careful physical attention, sometimes drifted into this condition of slow dying, while infants in the poorest homes, with a loving mother, often overcame the handicaps of poverty and unhygienic surroundings and became bouncing babies. It was found that the element lacking in the sterilized lives of the babies of the former class, and generously supplied to those that flourished in spite of hit-or-miss environmental conditions, was mother love. In consequence of this new insight, science, without attempting to analyze the life-giving quality of mother love, came to terms with instinct. Hospital authorities began looking around for a "Pharaoh's daughter" who could care for the threatened children who fell into their hands. A new system of carefully selecting foster mothers was developed, and, whenever an infant had no suitable person to care for him, he was sent to a foster home rather than to an institution. Young infants are now kept in hospitals for as short a time as possible. As a result marasmus has become a rare disease.

It is shocking that our ignorance endangered, through neglect of the human element of mothering, the lives of many infants we were trying to save, just at a time when science was making so much progress in other directions; yet the study of marasmus has added greatly to our understanding of infant nature. The disease showed in a dramatic way the meaning of the need for mothering experiences and the effect on the child's mental growth, as well as physical welfare, when this need was not satisfied. The typical life story of a baby who suffered from marasmus will help to make this clear.

Little Bob was born in the maternity hospital where the writer was making studies of infants at the time. He was a full-term child and weighed six pounds three ounces at birth. During his stay in the hospital, the baby was breast-fed and there was no apparent difficulty with his body functions. The mother, a professional woman, had been reluctant about breast-feeding because she wished to take up her work as soon as possible after the baby was born, but she yielded to the kindly encouragement of the hospital nurses, and the feeding was successful. Both mother and child were thriving when they left the hospital.

On returning home, the mother found that her husband had suddenly deserted her, the climax of an unhappy and

maladjusted marriage relationship. She discovered soon after that her milk did not agree with the baby. As is frequently the case, deep emotional reactions affect milk secretion. The infant refused the breast and began to vomit.
Later he was taken to the hospital and the mother did not
call to see him. At the end of a month she wrote that she
had been seriously ill and asked the hospital to keep the
child until further notice.

In spite of careful medical attention and skillful feeding,
this baby remained for two months at practically the same
weight. He was in a crowded ward and received very little
personal attention. The busy nurses had no time to mother
him and play with him as a mother would, by changing his
position and making him comfortable at frequent intervals. The habit of finger-sucking developed, and gradually
the child became what is known as a ruminator, his food
coming up and going down with equal ease. At the age of
two months he weighed five pounds. The baby at this time
was transferred to a small children's hospital, with the idea
that this institution might be able to save his life by giving
him more individual care. It became apparent that the
mother had abandoned the child altogether.

When seen by the writer, this baby actually looked like
a seven-months' foetus, but with a strange appearance of
oldness. His arms and legs were wrinkled and wasted, his
head large in proportion to the rest of the body, his chest
round and flaring widely at the base over an enormous
liver. His breathing was shallow, he was generally inactive
and listless, and his skin was cold and flabby. He took large

quantities of milk, but did not gain weight, since most of it went through him with very little assimilation and with copious discharges of mucus from his intestines. The baby showed at this time the pallor which, in our study, we have found typical of infants who are not mothered.

There was no definite evidence of organic disease, but growth and development were definitely at a standstill, and it appeared that the child was gradually slipping backward to prenatal levels of body economy and function.

The routine treatment at the new hospital for the baby who is not gaining weight is to give him concentrated nursing care. He is held by the nurse for all feedings and allowed at least half an hour to take the bottle. From time to time his position in the crib is changed, and, when possible, the nurse carries him about the ward for a few minutes before or after each feeding. This is the closest possible approach to mothering in a busy infants' ward. Medical treatment consists of frequent injections of salt solution under the skin to support the weakened circulation in the surface of the body and prevent dehydration.

With this treatment, Little Bob began to improve slowly. As his physical condition became better, it was possible for our research group to introduce the services of a volunteer "mother," who came to the hospital twice daily to give him more of the attention he so greatly needed. What she actually did was to hold him in her lap for a short period before feedings. She was told that he needed love more than he needed medicine, and she was instructed to stroke the child's head gently and speak or sing softly to

him and walk him about. Her daily visits were gradually
prolonged until she was spending an hour twice a day, giving the baby this artificial mothering. The result was good.
The child remained in the hospital until he was five
months of age, at which time he weighed nine pounds. All
rumination and diarrhea had stopped, and he had become an alert baby, with vigorous muscular activity. His
motor coordinations were, of course, retarded. Although
he held up his head well and looked about, focusing his
eyes and smiling in response to his familiar nurses, he
could not yet grasp his bottle or turn himself over, as is
customary at this age. The finger-sucking continued, as is
usually the case with babies who have suffered early privation.

In accordance with the new hospital procedure, as soon
as the child's life was no longer in danger, he was transferred to a good, supervised foster home in order that he
might have still more individual attention. Under this re-
gime, his development proceeded well and he gradually
mastered such functions as sitting, creeping, and standing.
His speech was slow in developing, however, and he did
not walk until after the second year. The general health of
this child was excellent at the end of his third year; also his
I.Q. was high on standard tests, but his emotional life was
deeply damaged. With any change in his routine or with a
prolonged absence of the foster mother, he would go into a
state quite similar to a depression. He became inactive, ate
very little, had intestinal disturbances, and was extremely
pale. When his foster mother was away, he usually reacted

with a loss of body tone and alertness, rather than with a definite protest. His emotional relationship to her was receptive, like that of a young infant, but he made little response to her mothering activities except to function better when she was there. He had little capacity to express affection, displayed no initiative in seeking it, yet failed to thrive without it. This lack of response made it difficult for the foster mother to show him the consistent love which he so deeply needed. Without the frequent friendly explanations of the situation by the visiting nurse, she would probably have given up the care of the child.

This story, an exaggerated example of what can happen to unmothered babies, throws light on both the physical and psychological importance of mothering. We have been too long inclined to see this only as a nursing problem, involving routine physical care, and not as an innate need of the child for a loving relationship.

The woman who is herself emotionally healthy, senses by instinct and can soon learn by observation to know her own baby. She will watch with keen interest for the progressive phases of his psychological growth and will also take the trouble to learn a few of the guideposts by which she can help in a smooth progress from one stage to the next. The essence of motherhood is creativeness, which is an instinctual gift. There are no set rules for the making of a great painting or the writing of a fine book or the composing of a great sonata. Yet a technique must be mastered. The depth of feeling which goes into creativeness cannot be measured out or indicated. This is determined by instinct. But whether mothering is done by instinct or design, it is important to know that it is as vital to the child's development as is food. The goal of the mother is to establish a positive relationship on which her leadership and training will depend. It is the means by which the infant learns cooperation and obedience and also develops a feeling of growth satisfaction. He becomes gradually assured that he is neither a toy nor an idol, but a developing individual who is adjusting to something that is good.

When we observe closely a large number of newborn babies to find out how ready they are to adapt to life, we are struck immediately by their helplessness. Many breathe insecurely and irregularly during the first weeks of life. Their bodies do not adjust to cold, and they shiver and turn bluish if exposure continues more than a few minutes. About 50 percent of those studied in our research needed help to establish sucking activity. Their repertory of behavior is limited to random wriggling and kicking movements and to paroxysmal crying. Much of the time they are in a sleeplike state, and if moved abruptly, they give a startle reaction. This is evidence that the nervous system is incomplete and the brain is not yet ready to function in control of behavior. Even instinctual behavior is muted in contrast to that of simpler mammals.

It has always seemed paradoxical that most young animals can satisfy their primal hungers at birth or soon after without much assistance. The opossum, for example, very low in the scale of mammals, climbs into the pouch of the mother immediately after birth and may even compete with another member of the litter for a nipple, to which he fastens himself and remains clinging. The rhesus monkey, much higher in the scale of mammalian development, often assists with his own birth by catching onto the hair of the mother and pulling himself out of the birth canal, after which he climbs to the breast and clings with arms around her body or neck. Yet our human babies are not able to reach for mother until they are four or five months old.

This paradox, however, is not really so surprising. Just because these animals have a much simpler brain and nervous system, they are more mature at birth. Agility of locomotion is one of the highest accomplishments of this monkey. While human babies, who have vastly higher potentialities, cannot function for themselves until certain areas of the brain become fully developed. In order that this maturing may take place, two conditions which were not possible before birth are necessary, namely, a more constant and adequate supply of oxygen for brain growth and the contact experiences of mothering, which gradually help to awaken sensory activity and awareness. These two factors constitute the basis for establishing the growth of the brain.

A baby does not come into the world complete, a small-scale adult. The early painters took a long time to discover that a child does not look like a miniature man or woman, and some of their paintings of madonna and child are amusing to us for that reason. But we ourselves are even more obtuse when we think of a child's mental and nervous organization as being like that of an adult but on a small scale. The period of brain growth in the first year of life is rapid and intense. Much of its substance, particularly the gray matter, is quite incomplete at birth; the cells are unfinished and some of the blood vessels which feed and irrigate them are not yet developed. It is for this reason that the psychological role of the mother in helping to adjust is so important. Very few mothers know, and not too many scientists seriously concern themselves with the fact of this great immaturity of the human nervous system and the consequent helplessness and vulnerability of the infant. The baby is a potential person, but in the beginning is quite helpless, and his mother must actually function for him for many weeks. Any sudden separation from her at this time causes psychological trauma. The gradual gearing together of mother-child activities on a comfortable and pleasant basis definitely furthers the growth of the nervous system and gives the brain time to develop without stress.

2

Oxygen Hunger

THE BABY's first cry is awaited with great interest. Probably never again in his lifetime will his vocal self-expression be listened to with so much absorption and relief. In fact, so dramatic is the birth cry, so sudden and clear and reassuring, that it is apt to be interpreted at too mature a level. Parents and relatives, their hopes realized, usually infer from it that breathing is a function that is now well established and self-regulating. Now, in any such cheerful conclusions, there is both truth and error. When the newcomer slips off the ways into life's sea, his breathing motors are incomplete and at times incapable of regular functioning; weeks may pass before he can be allowed to venture from shore. In other words, it is true, of course, that the wailing infant breathes, but this he may do with inadequacy. He has at birth an inner adjustment to make to his new environment which is somewhat like that of the astronaut or the deep-sea diver. He must have help and must exercise to keep his breathing mechanisms running smoothly.

Physiologically we know that the first cry is an emergency form of breathing. In the beginning, it is mostly a bellowslike action of the diaphragm which serves alter-

nately to expel any remaining fluids from the lungs and to
suck in oxygen. The sound element at this time is largely
incidental and is in all probability due to an automatic
valvelike action of the vocal cords as the air passes in and
out.

An actual breathing dilemma may confront the baby at
birth, perhaps a uniquely human dilemma. As the eminent pediatrician and physiologist Professor Joachim
Brock, of Marburg, has expressed it, long ago; "The young
suckling child lives constantly in a condition of 'physiological insufficiency of breathing.' " * Despite the fact that
oxygen is plentiful in the air, the infant may continue to
be in want because of the immaturity of the breathing ap-
paratus and also because his body is adjusted to breathing
by way of that highly important prenatal organ, the
placenta.

Mothering is the important factor which helps in
breaking this deadlock, so we see once more that dependence on the mother seems to have roots in a basic biological activity—respiration.

To appreciate the nature of the breathing dilemma at
birth and to understand why it is peculiar to mankind, we
must study some complicated facts of human development.

Scientists have recently learned from important research that the brain's internal breathing, or metabolism,
is more intense during early growth than at any time;
moreover, that part of the brain which is characteristically

* Brock, *Biologische Daten für den Kinderarzt* (Berlin, Springer, 1932)
II, 9.

human, the so-called gray matter, requires twice as much oxygen as other tissues for development. Obviously, then, there must be an increasing demand for this essential element in the first months of life.

The prenatal baby, having no access to the outer air, gets his oxygen from the placenta through the blood. This ration (another shaft of inquiry reveals) becomes scant as his nervous system begins to mature toward birth. Blood analysis shows that the young baby who is unmothered, somewhat like a person living in an extremely high altitude, often endures in his new environment a condition of oxygen-want. This may be one of the causes for frequent crying.

Man's brain, in maturity his greatest asset for survival, seems to be a burdensome liability while he is making his entrance into the world. The offspring of the lower mammals, though they share the vulnerability of our young to mechanical birth injury, are probably immune to this more subtle danger; their brain development is less complex and hence uses so little oxygen that a temporary lack of it causes no significant damage.

Also, after birth the human brain is for many months a burdensome possession, making the child, in a biological sense, property poor. Its upkeep and growth take a lion's share of the developing body's oxygen supply. Yet, the lungs must develop further before there can be adequate intake of air. The chest itself at birth is often barrel-shaped, with its tiny intercostal muscles unable to assist with breathing. It cannot rise and fall with each breath because of its peculiar structure; the ribs, flaring widely at the waistline to accommodate the liver beneath, either run horizontally or tilt slightly upward. Thus, for many weeks, the baby's chest is fixed.

It was once believed that the first cry was an indication that the infant suddenly had made the change from the vegetative life within the mother to adequate air breathing. We know now that the process of adjustment to a new environment takes time. Actually, the way is long and development is slow, hence human infancy is a highly vulnerable period. Another factor which we must now consider is the persistence of prenatal physiology which tends to outlast its usefulness. This happens more often than we might think. The newborn cannot unlearn in a moment what he has been practicing for months!

As has been recently established, definite respiratory movements occur while the child is still inside the uterus. Obviously this is not air breathing, since the foetus lives in a liquid environment and the chief source of oxygen is the maternal placenta. At this time the blood is the breathing medium. What does occur is this. A small amount of oxygen is taken up in the blood cells of the baby's liver, which before birth is a blood-making organ and also acts somewhat like a lung, receiving freshly oxygenated blood from the placenta. The muscle of the diaphragm arches over it, cup-fashion, and exerts suction on this oxygen supply. This action is thought to draw fresh blood upward toward the developing lungs and brain. Certain body movements of the baby—twisting, flexion, and extension of the torso before birth and after birth the familiar wriggling—probably assist the diaphragm with this circulatory function.

Occasionally, this prenatal form of respiration can be observed when immediately after birth infants fail to breathe until the cord is tied. What we see in these rare cases is spasmodic upward suction movement of the diaphragm, with flattening of the abdomen. This is followed by relaxation with marked protrusion or the abdomen as air flows into the lungs and crowds down the liver and intestines. Some understanding of prenatal breathing explains what would otherwise seem a strange paradox.

Early crying consists then of a series of more or less violent expirations. When the newborn is not crying, breathing is at times shallow and rapid. It is often impossible to count, but mechanical recordings show that here, too, expirations are more prolonged than the sorely needed inspirations. One would naturally expect the latter to predominate, in view of the baby's known oxygen hunger. Only on the basis of past performance does this behavior make any sense at all. After birth, the muscle of the diaphragm is learning to reverse itself, to suck downward and draw air into the lungs, after months of upward suction. Of course, such a drastic change as this takes time. It also takes time for the previously static chest to acquire an active role.

The baby is hampered indeed, then, by all the factors which we have now considered. We come next to the crux of the matter—what can be done to help him? In what way can mothering facilitate his breathing?

Obviously, a mother cannot teach her baby to breathe.

She cannot show him how to abandon any vestige of foetal technique, how to expand his lungs and make respiration secure until the all-important brain centers which insure its performance are more mature.

What is it that mothering accomplishes? What she can do is to furnish the stimulus which is necessary to bring important reflex mechanisms into action. It so happens that the baby's first response to her touch is respiratory. It happens that her handling automatically initiates deeper inspiration and helps in its establishment. From being held, fondled, allowed to suck freely and frequently, the child receives reflex stimulation, which primes his breathing mechanisms into action and which finally enables the whole respiratory process to become organized under the control of his own nervous system.

There is an ancient belief, still current, that babies who sleep with the mother are in danger of suffocation. This bit of folklore is for the most part a reversal of truth. Since the contact is a protection rather than a peril to the infant, he sleeps more safely in the first weeks at his mother's side than in the stimulus-free seclusion of a modern nursery. In certain continental hospitals, where this fact is appreciated, each maternity bed has a small basket attached to it so that the newborn baby is never for a moment beyond his mother's reach. Consistent personal attention is vitally important.

We have used the word "important" advisedly. Perhaps the reader wonders why it is important for mothering to hasten the baby across the bridge, in lieu of letting him choose his own unhurried pace. There are several reasons.

In the first place, if prenatal breathing persists, a state of inanition may occur. Although for a short time after birth, the child has two sources of oxygen—the outer air and his own tissues—he must not rely too long on the latter source, which is meager and fast diminishing. In the second place, prolonged oxygen shortage may produce brain damage not evident at the time, but of peculiar importance to future mental life.

This is the story: While outer breathing is being established, so also is the inner breathing, or metabolism, of the nervous system; this inner breathing depending on the outer, of course, for its oxygen supply. Now if the baby's respiration fails to develop on schedule, metabolism must operate on short rations and the growing cells of the brain may suffer in consequence. The caliber of developing blood vessels may not become sufficient for the irrigation of nerve cells; the myelin sheaths which protect and nourish the nerve fibers may not complete themselves; brain metabolism itself may become established on a poor basis. Such handicaps as these can make an individual biologically unfit to meet the stress and strain of later life. In other words, his subsequent ability to "take it" may hang in the balance during this early period.

The importance of mothering in helping the child to breathe at this time can hardly be stressed too greatly. As to the amount of stimulation optimal for breathing—here the average vigorous child himself makes certain lusty announcements, for it happens that excessive crying is significant in this connection.

The quiet baby has to be watched with special care. He

may be too weak to cry. Early crying is largely a breathing exercise, simply the child's automatic adjustment to postnatal respiration, and consequently one or two spells a day are of distinct advantage. However, if crying periods continue for longer than five or ten minutes, an investigation should be made immediately, and some simple measure used to soothe and comfort—stroking the child's head, allowing him to suck on a clean pacifier, or carrying him about—usually will relieve the condition. Tipping his head down may help to bring a fresh supply of oxygenated blood to the brain.

Therefore, it is important to note in the first months of life the breathing and crying of a baby, which are invaluable indicators, as they show whether his life schedule is actually answering his oxygen needs. The advice, "let baby cry it out," does not apply until much later. Infants should be soothed promptly, since the crying of the first weeks signifies emergency breathing.

At last comes the day of respiratory independence, and the infant himself announces the fact! Amusingly enough, his first babbling syllables, however meaningless they may be according to usual standards of speech, do tell us one thing: that an inner balance of oxygen has been reached. No longer so dependent on the touch of the mother for stimulation, the baby himself is able to experiment with and exercise for himself his newfound breathing abilities and he does this through vocalization, a mutual delight to himself and to his mother. Another indicator of this novel and delightful state of freedom is the smile which often precedes or accompanies babbling and which seems to mean release of tension.

Some babies who have had wise and consistent mothering begin to vocalize in the second month. Others who have been left too much alone or else have been inconsistently handled are delayed in development until much later. These unfortunate infants may have trouble in their speech development and are slow in talking. In our study we found a definite correlation in some cases between the development of talking and adequacy of early care; not only did the well-mothered babies vocalize sooner but also their speech maintained a smoother and easier progress.

Such facts as these show that the story of learning to breathe does not end with the baby's achievement of respiratory independence but continues through this interesting and complicated process of learning to talk. There is a close relationship between breathing, sucking, and speech.

To bring into practical use the somewhat complicated facts introduced in this chapter, let us summarize:

1. "Mothering" a newborn baby helps him to breathe more adequately by bringing into action certain nervous reflexes which insure proper and necessary respiration.

2. This early oxygen intake is a factor in starting the fires of life in the rapidly developing brain cells; hence, it is one of the first steps toward mental functioning.

3. Good breathing is a factor in smooth speech development and is throughout life closely related to both physical and mental health.

3

Sucking

IN THIS CHAPTER, the author is faced with a problem, and the problem is the reader, who may think, like many of the parents connected with the infant study, that the subject of sucking is a distasteful one to consider and discuss. It is particularly important, however, in this instance, to see the child as an incomplete individual who has his own ways of functioning and may be having a hard time developing and getting used to his new kind of life. If he does not begin to function according to Nature's plan, he is not going to feel well in the next stages of development. His sucking may be a primitive and revolting activity to fastidious parents, but when the many aspects of this first mouth activity are understood its importance becomes clear.

A baby's mouth is the center of his universe, the avenue through which hunger and thirst are assuaged, tension reduced, and comfort restored. He experiences his first important taste of his new life and his first grasp through sucking, which is innate biological endowment. During the first six months, it is the infant's most satisfying and all-absorbing activity and the one in which he becomes a wholehearted participant with his mother.

Unfortunately most people consider sucking as merely the baby's way of digesting his food. They think of the mouth with its delicate sensitivity and elaborate muscular equipment as simply the upper end of the digestive tract. The fact that I wish to emphasize, however, is that this function, aside from the intake of nourishment, satisfies important psychological needs. When sucking has become well established, made easy, and exercised freely, any observer can see that the child is getting satisfaction, and this is true of a young infant whether or not an appreciable amount of fluid is ingested. It has been found in the hospital routine of weighing a baby before and after nursing, to estimate how much food he gets, that many infants in the first weeks of life nurse quite contentedly without getting any quantity of milk. The mouth activity has relieved tension, and a beginning relationship with the mother is forming. Another important aspect of oral activity is that it brings a better supply of blood to the head and face, probably to the brain itself, thus contributing to the progressive development of that organ.

The immediate pleasure value of his mouth activity to the infant himself is easy to see from his reaction. Pleasure is the principle on which he accepts or rejects; at this age it is his criterion of good and bad, and no Emily Post is going to make him pretend anything different. Sucking reaches a maximum intensity about the fourth month of life, and if it has been fully and agreeably exercised up to this time its urgency tends to diminish somewhat as the child begins to vocalize, to bite, and to grasp with his hands. The close relationship among these functions in the first months of life may easily be seen. Looking ahead, we must realize that speech, which will be the main expression of mental activity, is closely related to this early mouthing.

It is an interesting fact that primitive people have always sensed intuitively the importance for babies of the immediate establishment of sucking. The Sioux Indians, for example, prepare a berry juice which they give to the child at frequent intervals during the first twenty-four hours to stimulate the mouth and relieve thirst. When the secretion of the mother's breast is thought to be established and the baby becomes restless and shows some mouthing activity, an old woman of the tribe, who is designated for this particular rite, rubs the inside of the infant's mouth with her fingers to prepare for the initial act of sucking.

A custom which is performed at all births among certain tribes of South Africa is described by Laubscher: "As soon as the child is born, it is given first some special medicine and thereafter put to the breast. This is a dramatic moment, for should the baby refuse to drink, the mother is suspected of being associated with witchcraft. If the child behaves normally at the breast, the custom of Futwa is performed. The branches from a tree called Minikandiba are put on a fire in a spot where the woman was confined and not in the recognized fireplace in the center of the hut. If the child cries, the smoke is considered to have a beneficial effect." * Intuitively, these people have instituted rites

* Barend F. J. Laubscher, *Sex Customs and Psychopathology* (New York, McBride, 1938), chap. IV, p. 68.

which help the infant get the use of this first behavior co-ordination between sucking and breathing. Our modern civilization does not emphasize the vital signficance of this basic phase of infant development unless an infant has serious difficulty in the establishment of his sucking reflex, and no provision is made for its frequent and rhythmical exercise. Perhaps we unconsciously try to hurry the infant over a period which seems to us too primitive. Our infants may suffer from the false delicacy which makes the very word "sucking" something perverted and to be avoided.

If we summarize briefly what the embryologist has to tell us about the way in which the mouth develops in human beings, it will help to explain how so many functions are fused in early oral activity. The lining of the oral cavity is developmentally a part of the skin which has become folded in to form a pouch. This indicates that the mouth is fundamentally an organ of touch. Its nerve supply comes directly from the brain through five different cranial nerves. In the first weeks of foetal development, nose and mouth are one cavity, separated from the digestive tract by a membrane which some time later breaks through and disappears. The mouth is thus in the beginning a large pocket just beneath the brain, with which it is connected much more closely than it is with the stomach.

The hard palate, which will separate the nose and mouth, begins to develop at about the sixth week of intra-uterine life. This structure is peculiar to mammals and plays the important role of dividing the mouth into an eating and breathing compartment. It might be compared with the diaphragm, also a structure peculiar to mammals, which separates the chest cavity from the abdomen.

The tongue muscle, which is to be the chief organ for sucking and later for speaking, begins to develop in the embryo while the mouth and nose are one continuous cavity. Its origin is very close to that of the heart, and its fibers are somewhat like those of the heart muscle. It is located first directly over the main artery to the head, suggesting that its original function has to do with pumping blood supplies toward the brain. In its development it migrates upward into the floor of the mouth and begins to take on new functions. Its first activity, upward pumping, is directly the reverse of sucking and swallowing. This action is sometimes seen in premature babies who have difficulty in establishing postnatal sucking. It is also seen in Mongolian idiots who frequently protrude and retract the tongue.

The tactile function of this important organ begins about the seventh month of foetal life. Its pumping action brings it back and forth across the sensitive hard palate, and this may be the first direct tactile experience of the individual. The tongue thus has various functions in the course of its development. Its intimate connection with the brain and its relation to early mental life, through speech, is evident from the variety of cranial nerves which supply it. The nerves which supply the tongue, the diaphragm, and the sensory lining of the mouth are all correlated in the sucking reflex, and around this important mechanism the sensory life of the infant develops.

Sucking is then a part of the instinctual behavior with

which the child is equipped at birth. Some babies suck vigorously on their fingers as soon as the head is delivered, and this activity recurs at more or less rhythmical and frequent intervals. Nursing is no problem to them. However, the spontaneous mouthing movements which are present in some infants at birth are not always coordinated. Many infants when placed at the breast for the first time fail to respond with effective coordinated sucking. This can be disconcerting to a young mother, who may think of herself as a failure or that there is a defect in the child. Several guided performances may be necessary before either breast- or bottle-feeding develops into the vigorous and effective activity characteristic of the well-adjusting baby. In the group of six hundred infants studied in our research, at least 40 percent had to be helped to suck in the following manner: The mouth had to be opened, the nipple inserted well inside the mouth cavity, and the chin of the baby worked rhythmically up and down by the nurse or mother.

What actually does this maneuver accomplish? Fundamentally, it brings about a simultaneous stimulation by the nipple of the upper surface of the tongue and of the hard palate. This stimulus is at times necessary to activate that important part of our nervous equipment known as the sucking reflex. Without assistance on the part of the mother to insure this kind of oral stimulation, the first sucking of the child can be ineffectual and slow to develop into the all-absorbing performance with which we are familiar.

It is the custom among European peasants to place a

pacifier in the child's mouth immediately after birth. If done judiciously, this is an excellent stimulus for the sucking reflex. In this country, the Negro mammies of the Old South made a great ceremony of preparing a "sugar rag" for the coming infant. This was made of bread crumbs and sugar tied in a soft piece of old linen cloth and moistened before being put into a baby's mouth. These Negro women sometimes gave their own babies a piece of fat bacon, thoughtfully tied to a string in order to retrieve it should it be swallowed! In this way they stimulated sucking and helped the infant to get satisfaction from his first adaptation to life outside the uterus. The wisdom in this traditional custom is shown by the fact that infants in the care of these Negro mammies very rarely had difficulty in the immediate establishment of this function. In this way the baby is given advance practice in the art of sucking before food hunger becomes too urgent.

Another specific reaction to vigorous sucking is seen in the respiration of the baby, which was emphasized in the last chapter. Shallow and irregular in the beginning, it deepens with the sucking, and the tendency to frequent paroxysmal crying diminishes. The muscle tension of the child relaxes temporarily during the sucking, and random movements are quieted. The color and temperature of the skin improve. The sleep which follows well-established sucking is the beginning of true body rest and not the uneasy semiconsciousness which characterized the newborn child.

Very quickly, rhythmic intervals become established in

which the infant shows evidence of the beginning of a "need to suck," and in close relation it can be seen that a certain alertness or awareness is developing.

How do we know, then, that this change in the child is definitely connected with sucking and is not due to inner developmental processes? Chiefly because babies who have trouble with the establishment of sucking invariably show a disorganization of these same physiological activities, that is, breathing, circulation, and muscle tone. When, in order to give quickly to a poorly nourished child sufficient quantities of nutriment to maintain weight, a medicine dropper or tube is used, the infant so fed is listless and has a distressed or pinched look and is inclined to remain, much of the time, in a half-conscious state. When the usual mouth action is absent and the child is entirely passive, even the absorption of the food is poor. This form of feeding is only a makeshift and cannot be continued over long periods without damage to the nervous reflexes of the mouth. Premature infants who are artificially fed in this way must later be taught to suck.

Toward the end of the second month, we can see that sucking has become associated with other sensory activities. The most striking connection—and one very pleasing to the mother—is with the eyes. Most babies nurse at first with the eyes unfocused. The eyes show little tendency to fixate for more than a fleeting moment. As sucking becomes easy and gratifying, the infant begins to show "eye attention." First he appears to look at the face of his mother, which at this time probably registers only as a patch of light moving about. (However, she has a flattered feeling that she is being noticed.) Somewhat later, the baby looks for the breast. When the eyes have begun to fixate quite definitely and to follow the movements of the mother for periods of several seconds, an important moment has arrived—the eyes begin to share with the mouth in this relationship, the first of life.

As the mother talks or sings to the child, the sound of her voice also becomes associated with nursing. By the end of the third month, in cases where no disturbance has occurred in the nursing relationship, the infant turns his head at the approach of the mother and looks at her, often giving a fleeting smile of satisfaction—her reward! (And, at least, more than the demanding nestlings ever accord to their overworked parents.) But she knows, and close chronological study of these progressive reactions indicates, that through the medium of the mother's person and the delicate assistance which she gives, elaborate functional associations are assisted to develop in the baby's brain. Babies who do not have consistent mothering are definitely slower in development and less alert. They do not seem to understand as well, later on, such simple matters as loving and being loved.

As the process of touch, sight, and hearing thus become integrated with the mouth activity, the hands and arms begin to coordinate and reach out and grasp. It is well known that from birth the hands have a tendency to seek the mouth in a haphazard fashion. In order that feeding may not be interrupted, the mother often holds the free hand of the baby away from his mouth. The baby automatically clasps and unclasps his hand around her finger. Later on, while he is sucking, he may feel or reach for the mother's finger, his own ear or nose, or some part of his clothing, and this associated behavior assists the hand in assuming its later touching and grasping function. Around three to five months, in well-mothered babies, the uncoordinated movements of the hand and arm have begun to give way to definite reaching and grasping activities, and some babies reach their arms definitely toward the mother.

Mouth grasping and hand grasping in this early period, and for some months of life, are practically interchangeable. The infant explores the universe with mouth as well as hand. Give the child a toy and into his mouth it goes, giving us the false impression that all he cares about is, "Is it good to eat?" We forget that as our fingers by just closing around an object give us a quick "feel" of its shape and texture, so the baby's mouth, more experienced than his fingers, can take in a new shape and surface. It is not unusual to see a year-old child reach for something with his mouth if his hands are engaged, and it is later in his development that he makes distinctions between food and play objects. Thus a close association exists between hand grasping or groping and the development of the first sensory grasping. It is significant that we use the same verb for both processes. It seems highly probable that sucking is the primitive biological activity which serves as a foundation for the development of the infant's emotional hold on the mother, his curiosity and orientation toward inanimate objects, and finally his dawning recognition of those other realities which are the basis of his learning. He drinks in with eyes and ears, along with milk, as he stares and listens. Later he will be able to learn words and express some of the feelings by way of the mouth. In this way, the early mouth experiences contribute to the development of speech. The child will later handle words as names or symbols for persons and objects; this is true mental expression. In infants whose sucking activities are limited and who do not receive the mothering which stimulates response in the sense organs, speech is definitely retarded.

Many modern pediatricians hold that a healthy, well-developed baby digests his food better if he is not fed frequently, so that the stomach completely empties itself and has a period of rest (so does mother). A few maternity hospitals adhere to the three-hour interval for meals. The majority, however, use four-hour intervals, and in some cases the attempt has been made to put fairly young babies on three meals a day. It is possible to do this without too much privation and nervous consequences, provided the infant is given water in the interval and is allowed to suck sufficiently so that he gets both oral and gastrointestinal exercise. However, it was found in our studies that young babies on the three-hour schedule were organized better and much less restless than those fed less often, even though both received an identical amount of food. In the baby, the tension of waiting for food is not as great as the nervous tension created by insufficient mouth activity. In other words, infants cannot live by food alone. And right here, we reach a place where we must stop and do some careful thinking, for it is clear that the problem of the mother is not only to satisfy food needs of a baby but to help him feel secure and to understand him as a human being who needs to be loved. His readiness to cooperate and later to follow and obey his parents' leadership into more mature ways hinges on this first piece of cooperation with mother.

An attempt was made to differentiate between the baby's food hunger and stimulus hunger in order to determine how much actual sucking exercise is necessary for the child's well-being, as well as how much food he requires. This was done by weighing breast-fed infants before and after feeding, and by timing the spontaneous sucking activity. It was found that two hours a day was the minimum oral exercise in the well-developed baby, while immature or premature infants needed a great deal more. This minimum, when used as a basis for feeding, from after the first week of life until the fourth month, would mean six meals a day, lasting approximately twenty minutes each. If the child ingested his food in less than twenty minutes, it was found he invariably sucked his fingers afterward for sufficient mouth exercise.

The mouth of the baby must have special consideration as an organ, the use and stimulation of which arouses the first sense of well-being and pleasure and definitely furthers his early sense of relationship. At the same time, however, it must be remembered that babies who are not held and fondled, or normally mothered, show excessive sucking habits and frequently take too much food, thereby bringing about digestive upsets as a natural result. They may become withdrawn or else antagonistic. This is particularly true of bottle-fed babies who must be regarded as deprived individuals, unless the mother succeeds in showing her love through other forms of attention.

The experiment was tried of giving a group of babies rubber nipples or pacifiers as soon after birth as restless or mouthing movements were noticed. Some infants began to suck at once and their restlessness was immediately quieted. They relaxed, relinquished the nipple in a short time, and fell asleep. The sucking impulse was satisfied in the same way that food hunger is appeased by the ingestion of food. In no case did sucking develop into a habit, except in those infants who fell ill or for some reason were not getting enough satisfaction from mothering.

Since sucking is a function which is soon replaced, the best arrangement, where possible, is to follow Nature's cue. In normal breast-feeding, which is without question the ideal form, at least until the teething period, the various needs are self-regulated. The amount of flow of the mother's milk and the time and effort needed by the baby to extract it usually correspond nicely with his needs. The contact and fondling give the necessary passive stimulation.

Artificial feeding immediately introduces the necessity for a careful regulation of sucking time coordinated with the flow of milk from the bottle. Holding, before and during the bottle feeding, is obviously necessary.

From a chemical viewpoint alone, of course, enough evidence of the value of breast-feeding to the infant can be cited to establish thoroughly its superiority over bottle-feeding. But even in this regard, subtle factors are often overlooked. For instance, a breast-fed baby, if given breast milk in a bottle, will often refuse it, thus giving evidence that for the infant more is involved in breast-feeding that the simple ingestion of food.

From the emotional point of view, the subtle factor entering into the situation is the question of well-being and security. We know, in our own adult experience, that our food does not "agree" with us if we eat alone too often or under unpleasant conditions or if we are angry or worried. This same situation holds for infants only in greater degree. Children not infrequently refuse food altogether when mother is tense or angry or when they feel themselves unloved. When food is taken under such conditions, unquestionably digestion proceeds less successfully than under happy emotional circumstances. When we realize that an infant has little capacity at birth to get a sense of security except in the feeding relationship, we appreciate the strong emotional factor involved in the question.

Breast-feeding is the first satisfaction a child gets from his mother after birth. This pleasure immediately begins to establish a focus on the mother and prepares the ground for the fostering of a continually richer relationship between them. As a result, the breast-fed baby is better nourished and his emotional development is smoothed considerably. For, naturally, breast-fed babies tend to have more trust and confidence in their mothers and consequently are easier to lead, train, and direct.

Breast-feeding is the very essence of "mothering" and the most important means of immunizing a baby against that greatest of emotional hazards, anxiety.

Sucking, once again, is a developmental activity of the greatest importance to the infant. The mouth with its counterpart in the brain (the speech center) is the nucleus of self. And the primary factor enabling him to pass through this stage successfully is the same factor we have discovered in relation to other functions: the understanding love of the mother.

4

Premental Behavior

THE BABY is never a silent partner in the first relationship with his mother. He both propels himself and is propelled into a world which is completely unfamiliar, but he arrives equipped with a type of behavior which adapted him to the highly protected life within his mother's body. His inherited or unlearned patterns of action help to continue his development, but cannot yet adjust him to the outside world.

This first infant activity has had many interpretations. Parents and psychologists have made valiant attempts to explain it retrospectively, that is, by reading into it meaning taken from the behavior of the older child or adult. It has been called variously "defense behavior," "attack behavior," "flight behavior," or simply dismissed as "purposeless activity." These movements do seem purposeless insofar as grasp, locomotion, or other coordinated behavior is concerned, but, as we shall see, they have an immediate significance in aiding the circulation, while the heart is adjusting itself to the new way of living. These first movements are frequently called "mass behavior" because they involve the entire organism. The precise and well-special-

ized forms of activity which we know in the older child develop out of it.

Before birth, when the lungs and gastrointestinal tract
are not yet functioning, the random swimming-like movements of the baby serve to help circulation. They pump
through the small body and toward the rapidly developing
brain the nutriments and oxygen absorbed into the blood
stream from the placenta. Thus the first gross body movement which we come to think of later in terms of locomotion and other specific activities has to do primarily
with breathing and with the nourishment of all the body
tissues. Of the six-month infant it has been said that he
laughs and weeps with his entire body. Of the newborn
baby, we may say that he eats, breathes, and feels with his
entire body.

The vigorous arm waving, kicking, squirming, and head
turning of the newborn child thus aid materially in mobil-
izing food and oxygen supplies in the tissues and driving
them into the expanding capillaries of the lungs and brain.
It is well known that when the movements of a baby are
restricted—for example, by bandaging the arms to prevent
finger-sucking—a panic of hyperactivity as violent as if
breathing had actually been interfered with is the immediate result. The same sort of panic reaction takes place in
most babies if the head is firmly held so that its almost constant turning movements are restricted, and the majority
of healthy infants cry violently. It is evident that free play
of the muscles is necessary for the health and well-being of
the child. Where the old custom of swaddling is still prac-

ticed, it is an established fact that the infant must be wrapped up shortly after birth, or he will resist this in such a way as to make it difficult.

"I wonder what he is thinking." Almost every mother, perhaps from time immemorial, has said in some instance or other while looking fondly at the little baby in her arms. Yet all the evidence available would seem to lead to the conclusion that the child does not think at all during the first two or three months of his existence. It appears to be characteristic of the infant, that he must do a great deal of sensing and acting before he can think. The maxim to think before you act is reversed in infant behavior, which may be why we have to learn it with difficulty later. The child's first behavior is directed from within his body by instinct. It has to do with the primary inner hungers; it is also determined in the beginning by the pleasure-pain principle and contributes to his first feelings of self.

The first weeks of the infant's life represent an important period for developing a good circulation. During this time some of the blood vessels which functioned before birth become obliterated. The heart muscle itself develops rapidly and pumps blood in new directions. We have to remember that in the first weeks of life, the heart is not constructed as it is in adulthood. From its size, shape, and position before birth, we may draw the conclusion that its first function was partly that of a suction action which tended to draw the elements needed from the placenta and from the infant's liver, where they were temporarily stored, into its capacious stomachlike cavity. From here the blood was gradually extruded toward the chest and head, but the growing heart itself had first claim on the supplies for the body.

For this reason the muscles just after birth must help the blood to circulate. Even in later life our muscles retain something of that function, for, as the eminent physiologist Dr. Walter B. Cannon has emphasized, "The laboring muscles act as if they were outlying hearts receiving more blood when they work, and pumping that blood back to the central heart and to the lungs for refreshment and a new service." *

The chief goal of the baby's first behavior, then, is self-development at its simplest level. Rhythmical repetition of basic body activities must necessarily go on without interference until higher levels of the brain begin to mature. And until this maturation takes place, the mother must do his thinking for him; that is, by a judicious use of her loving attention she must stimulate and make provision for free and comfortable activities which he cannot set in motion for himself. He is unable to adapt to changes until the upper levels of the brain have completed the primary stages of organization.

The mother who appreciates how complicated is the process of learning to live will not attempt the futile task of trying to implant in her infant's mind in the first months of life ideas that belong to a far higher level of development. She will be thankful that he has the right primitive instincts and she will help them along. Even in the

* Cannon, *The Wisdom of the Body* (New York, Norton, 1932), p. 163.

minds of highly intelligent people, a good deal of confusion exists about this deep instinctual drive within the human organism to develop itself. The life instinct, known later as the instinct for self-preservation, is a natural force which is constantly at work. In the early phases of life, behavior has to do predominantly with inner organic adjustment and has very little to do with adapting to the particular culture in which the child is born. When we attempt to apply moral and social concepts of selfishness to an infant, we show complete misunderstanding of human nature in its beginnings. It is to be hoped that the baby is selfish, and that his selfish needs will be met. Babies who do not have full instinctual gratification in this early period tend to develop a self which is weak, and inadequate; whereas through full satisfaction of primal hungers and through full and free use of the muscles and senses, young humans tend to become self-secure and to gain self-control.

An actual incident will show how far astray the best intention may lead the adult who does not understand a child's needs.

A young mother, a woman of superior intelligence and fine character, was deeply engrossed in conversation with the writer about the development of her small son, aged two months. The time came for the infant to be taken up and he began to squirm and wail vigorously. Questioned as to why she did not attend to the baby, she replied in all seriousness: "I have begun to teach my son not to be selfish. He must learn to wait when something important is going on." This otherwise loving and conscientious mother failed to realize that the tension of waiting is for a young baby an actual threat to the stability of his entire organism. Learning to wait can be accomplished only when the brain has reached a considerable state of maturity. What this mother desired of her young son of two months might be a possibility at two years, but not earlier. It is a difficult matter to make clear to parents—that comfort and satisfaction involve not self-indulgence for the infant but, rather, the very existence of self and its growth. The baby's need must be gratified somehow. The sequel to the above story is significant. This particular baby soon began to find solace and to relieve tension by sucking the end of his blanket. He developed various difficulties due to the irritation of wool fibers in his nose, mouth, and intestinal tract, and also—still more serious—a fixation of the sucking habit. This began to dominate his behavior, causing a marked retardation in the development of other forms of gratification, and became the source of untold worry to his mother, bringing continual conflict between her and the child. Thus we see that this mother's well-intentioned discipline, at an inappropriate time of life, led not to the establishment of a more social type of behavior but to the prolonged use of a more primitive type of activity.

Unfortunately, the idea is still disturbing to many people that mental life is so closely linked to and so firmly rooted in primitive biological activity, such as sucking, breathing, and eliminating. These links between what is somatic and psychic have never been made sufficiently clear. The inner needs and tensions due to the growth of the brain and nervous system in infancy are poorly understood, and the beginnings of the emotional reactions and of the thinking process have never been sufficiently studied. Yet just these bio-psychological connections are highly important because the development of vital personality in the adult depends essentially on the way the premental hungers of the baby are satisfied and on the help he gets in bringing his own behavior mechanisms into self-controlled action so that he can later satisfy his emotional needs and further his own intellectual curiosity, or desire to know.

All the early drives of the infant become normally focused around her, the mother, and he turns to her with a need that should never be disregarded. In some natural way an adequate answer to this seeeking force brings out in him the capacity for recognition and the urge to know and love, and these are forces which can become as strong ultimately as the hunger that brought them to life.

5

Sleep

THE YOUNG BABY is popularly thought to sleep twenty hours out of the twenty-four. The half-conscious dozing of the newborn, however, is not really sleep in its mature sense; it is more nearly a continuation of the prenatal state. The average infant does not reach a stage of being actually awake except for brief periods during the first weeks of life. This stuporous condition is another indication that the brain cortex is not yet functioning to any appreciable extent and that its connection with the sense organs is incomplete. Certain inner developments are going on which utilize the energies of the small organism. The true sleep which we refer to when we say "He slept like a baby," is not seen until the child has given evidences that he is awake over long periods and capable of appropriate sensory responses; that is, that mental activity has begun to develop (such evidences are the smile of recognition; the head turned in response to sound; and the first reaching and grasping for something observed).

It appears, then, that true sleep is a rhythmic relaxation which follows the beginning of higher brain activity. It is a biological rest reaction, like the diastole of the heart, like the pause which follows breathing, and the various other rest periods which follow the normal function of any organ of the body. We see it first developing after the excitement of hunger and the satisfaction of sucking experience. Sleep follows a period of stimulation and excitement. It is also the rest made necessary by rapid bodybuilding and by that mental seeking and grasping activity which we call conscious attention. In the beginning, it is largely automatic.

Deep prolonged sleep, it is generally agreed, does not appear until after approximately the fourth month of life. The two main reasons for the first long periods of semiconsciousness are lack of development of the brain cells and their connecting nerve fibers and insufficient oxygen in the brain circulation to maintain it in active function.

Certain obvious body characteristics distinguish this early semiconsciousness from true sleep. The eyes are closed, but on careful inspection the eyeballs are frequently seen moving back and forth. The usual posture, if the infant is not tucked in too tightly, is similar to the prenatal position with the knees slightly drawn up and the head bent down over the chest, the arms usually flexed, and the hands closed. There is seldom complete relaxation except immediately after sucking. Periodic random movements are quite frequent.

Another posture which is infrequently seen, but does occur in babies who are thought to be normal, is that of hyperextension of the entire body, particularly of the neck and head. Nurses sometimes complain that it is impossible to dress or drape a young baby because the muscles are so tense. This posture in older children is associated with conditions in which there is poor circulation in the brain. In infants it is often accompanied by paleness of the skin and coolness of the hands and feet.

In true sleep the eyes are closed and the muscles of the eyeballs are relaxed so that movement is seldom seen. The body muscles are soft and flexible. The skin is usually rosy, moist, and warm. The posture is entirely plastic and adaptable. Perhaps the most outstanding factor is that breathing is now deep and regular, instead of shallow and irregular as it is in the first weeks.

The mother has to aid in establishing a balance between appropriate stimulation and rest in order that the baby may develop a healthy sleeping routine. The adult is usually able to control any tensions due to too little or too much stimulation, so that in a state of health he can adjust his sleeping time to his own convenience without great difficulty. But most young infants have to be given appropriate rhythmical stimulation to sleep well; that is, their stimulus hunger has to be appeased and their avenues of sensory intake have to be brought into an appropriate state of adjustment. The only way a baby can put himself to sleep is by sucking. If he has to resort to this activity constantly in early life, it easily becomes a fixed habit. It is far better for him if the mother supplies this very much needed stimulus and comfort by gently rocking the child or softly singing. This also helps to improve his sense of equilibrium, and to allay, in a way that is gently agreeable, the infant's innate fear of falling.

The cradle's value in the first months of life is discussed

in the following chapter, but along with its rhythmic swing, the lullaby holds a time-honored place as a means of helping the infant to establish his sleeping function. The great composers, who, like all geniuses, have a deep understanding of man's nature and needs, have written lullabies that have brought sleep to countless babies. One reason for this is the child's extreme sensitivity to sound. It has been established that even before birth the foetus responds to music. It seems that singing to the young infant soft, simple, rhythmical songs brings a sense of relief and security to his sensitive nervous system and feeds his stimulus hunger. There is, as it were, a need to "convince" the child that sound is a good thing when presented pleasingly. Without this gentle introduction to sound, many babies continue for an unduly long period to react with a startle to sudden and loud noises. This rhythmic pleasure stimulus also helps to avoid the overdevelopment of thumb-sucking.

What about the infant who has been overstimulated by too much mothering, and what effect has this on sleep? This is a vital matter, for if the rapidly developing sensorium—that is, the part of the forebrain which receives incoming sensory impressions—is overtaxed, one of two serious complications may follow. Either the child may develop a tendency to overactivity or he may withdraw into a stuporous or shocklike state, which is described in a later chapter.

It is all-important, then, that these stimulus experiences must always be intelligently controlled. First, it must be stressed that their continuation after the child has fallen asleep is disturbing rather than soothing. More complicated is the necessary recognition on the mother's part that the child is a developing individual whose needs are constantly changing. As his sensory functions come into use and become stabilized, he begins to satisfy his own need for stimulation, and he needs less rocking and singing.

It must also be remembered that the purpose of rocking and singing is to help the child become accustomed to the feelings of sound and motion and to the use of his own body functions, not to fix his attention on them as a means of pleasure getting. These comforting experiences of being put to sleep counteract certain vague innate fears of the infant and reassure him about sensory stimuli with which he is unfamiliar, but they are not ends in themselves.

Baby Rob is an example of a child who showed this need for rocking or some form of rhythmical stimulation to induce sleep. This child was ten months old when he was referred to our study group because of what his mother called "a peculiar rolling habit." He had apparently been a very good sleeper from the time of birth, but the mother had discovered, on coming home late one night, that the infant was rocking violently back and forth in the bed with his arms tightly clasped around the end of the blanket. Observation showed that this was a regular occurrence. She was greatly disturbed and immediately jumped to the conclusion that the baby had somehow been injured and that, as she put it, "there was something mentally wrong with the child." In giving information about the general development and routine care of this infant, she repeatedly emphasized the fact that she had never played with him, that he had never been rocked or jiggled, and that he had always been left alone in his own bed in the nursery to go to sleep by himself. The nursery, she insisted, was "perfectly quiet and entirely isolated from the rest of the house."

When the suggestion was made to this mother that it would be good for her to spend a few minutes holding and playing with the child at regular intervals before his feedings during the day, and particularly in the late afternoon, she was plainly horrified and explained that she had taken special care "not even to let the child's father see him late in the afternoon when he came home from business lest the baby become too excited." She was, however, willing to try the experiment of rocking the child to sleep at night to test the result. She also agreed to place a dim light in the nursery, so that if the child was restless he need not waken in a totally dark room.

The rolling habit, of course, did not immediately disappear under this treatment, but there was enough improvement in the general reactions of the child within a week to convince the mother that she should continue the procedure. With the dawning understanding of what was wrong with her baby, this mother, who was not only intelligent but loving, worked out an ingenious scheme for supplying the appropriate stimulation which was so greatly needed. At the end of his first year she reported that the rolling habit had entirely disappeared.

The words of some of the best-known lullabies give us insight into their biological and psychological implications. The familiar "Rockabye, baby, on the tree top" is a good illustration. Here the association of rocking and the fear of falling are clearly brought out. The well-known Brahms lullaby refers to the odor stimulus of flowers and the softness of the cover, all pleasant sensations.

Another example of an intuitive approach to the meaning of a child's sleep is the first prayer which older children are frequently taught to say when they are put to bed:

> Now I lay me down to sleep,
> I pray the Lord my soul to keep;
> If I should die before I wake,
> I pray the Lord my soul to take.

The biological principle in this age-old prayer is a very important one. The activity of the brain which is awake and functioning is highly protective, in that it furnishes nervous energy for maintaining the life activity of the organism. The temporary setting aside of consciousness during sleep causes a certain amount of apprehension in children who have not been mothered and in whom stimulus hunger has never been recognized and appeased. An older child for example, who is not getting enough mothering, invariably becomes apprehensive when he is put to bed. It means a painful separation. Staying awake unconsciously becomes to him a means of keeping watch against some vague danger. Many lullabies and prayers contain an assurance that the mother or the angels or some divine being is near at hand to protect the life of the child supposedly against external dangers. The real danger facing the un-loved child, of course, comes from the instability of his nervous system and the uneasiness that arises as a result of the imbalance of his body activities.

An illustration from the history of one of the children closely observed in our research will show a different angle of the sleep problem. Here this function became exaggerated as the child's means of escape from discomfort and frustration. From the beginning of life, Baby Pat had difficulty in sucking. This was due to the fact that her mother, a successful actress, was averse to breast-feeding. She weaned the child suddenly at the age of four weeks, and the infant was placed on infrequent bottle feedings. The actual food supply was entirely adequate, insofar as bulk and caloric intake were concerned, but the sucking time was too short and the infant had practically no mothering. The bottle was propped on a pillow, and the baby was not even held for feeding. Her response to this double frustration was the development of a tendency to sleep the greater part of the time. There was actually a slowing up of all sensory reaction, with a pronounced diminution in reflex excitability and a consequent depression of all body function. This child became extremely pale and lethargic, and at the age of six months was retarded in many aspects of her development. Apparently the thing which disturbed her the most was to be awakened, in response to which she would get into a panic of screaming and restlessness. For example, if she were drinking milk from the bottle and the nipple became stopped up or the flow of milk lessened because of the vacuum created in the bottle, she would immediately doze off without any protest reaction, and the bottle usually slipped to the floor with a crash. The child would then wake up and scream as if terrified. The usual means of soothing had little effect on her.

The only sure means of gratification for this infant was sleep, which was not actually sleep, but really an automatic withdrawal. This economy of function enabled her to maintain life by a sort of hibernation, and the interruption of this protective mechanism filled her with uncontrollable anxiety.

For a few months, contact with this child was lost because the mother felt that the advice given her was impractical, since it interfered with her professional duties. At the age of eleven months, the child was brought to the clinic by her father, who had become alarmed over her condition and realized that the baby's health was seriously threatened. When he brought her for advice, he related the following incident: the previous evening in the room where the child was asleep he had been reading and had climbed up on a stepladder to take down an encyclopedia from a high shelf. Accidentally, he let several volumes fall to the floor close to the infant's bed. Highly alarmed at the idea that she might have been struck, he hastened to pick her up, but found the baby so deeply asleep that she gave not the slightest reaction. (This child automatically utilized sleep as a flight or in avoidance of frustration.) When the father later related this incident to the mother, she assured him that this was deep and restful sleep which was normal for a baby. She was not aware of the pathological nature of the stupor and did not connect it with the general condition of the child.

It was several months before the sensitivity of this infant was restored and her stimulus-response mechanisms readjusted to healthy functional activity. This was brought about actually by the fortunate engagement of the services of an extremely motherly nurse, to whom the condition was explained. She recognized that this baby needed love and reassurance to regain her functional balance.

To sum up, sleep is, after the first weeks, the natural counterpart of outside stimulation and of inside conscious mental activity and has to be regulated in close connection with the other instinctual and growth needs. As we have already seen, the mechanisms through which the mind is to work and relax are being developed in the beginning of life and need careful consideration.

The best practical plan for an infant's sleeping arrangements, we found, after many observations, to be the following: In the first month in a cradle or carriage at his mother's side; after this time it is the right of every human child to have a room of his own for sleeping, preferably adjoining that of the parents. Until he is of school age his psychological growth requires this. The time for sleeping should be as invariable as possible and never less than sixteen hours a day in the first two years.

6

Learning to Feel

THERE IS MORE to say now about other kinds of sensitivity which relate the child to his environment and later contribute to feeling of self. The sense of touch, as we have already seen, is best developed in the mouth. The face and head are also extremely sensitive, and the gentle stroking of the head soothes a restless infant in a remarkable way. There is an old superstition that the head of a small baby should not be touched because of the fontanel, the so-called soft spot, where the skull bones are incompletely developed and where part of the brain surface on top of the head is covered only by the scalp. Some mothers are afraid to wash their babies' heads because of this! The infant could never stand the process of birth, if his head were so delicate.

In the general skin surface the sense of touch is not so well developed at birth, but is brought out through grooming and body care. From the time of the first bath, the entire skin surface needs this gentle stimulation. There is a great deal of discussion among obstetricians and pediatricians as to whether oil baths, soap and water baths, or no baths at all are better in the first weeks of life. The psychologist finds that the baby himself answers these questions in the response of general well-being which invariably follows, whether the bath is a warm dip or a body massage with an appropriate oil. Unless there is some skin disturbance present, cleansing is a secondary consideration at this time. The circulation and reflex activities definitely benefit by the gentle friction rub connected with the bath. If it were not for the attitude of nurses and mothers toward cleanliness, many babies would suffer actual neglect of this need for skin stimulation.

For wisdom, let us turn to the humbler animals. It is a matter of common observation that, beginning with birth, the cat mother licks her kittens all over several times a day. The mewing of the kitten immediately brings this attention and the cat mother is never long away from her offspring. Thoroughbred kittens who do not get this attention develop various functional disorders, such as vomiting, constipation, or diarrhea, and frequently die. The human mother is apt to read into these licking activities a purely cleansing implication. What she does not see is that it is a relational activity between mother and young which is important to both. This is similar to the primary relationship which biologists call symbiosis, through which Nature links together two organisms with mutual benefit. A cat deprived of her kittens will wander around restlessly for days, licking her owner or any available object. Frequently she adopts some young animal which may be at hand on which to lavish her maternal attention.

Scientists who have studied the grooming behavior of anthropoid apes report the same findings. The young in captivity who do not get this grooming care, but are for some reason separated from the parent apes, sicken and frequently die.

In a personal communication to the writer, the late Dr. Charles Stockard, of Cornell University, reported that puppies bred in his laboratories were unable to eliminate until they had been licked all over by the mother. Valuable animals separated too early from the mother were lost in this way, because the keepers did not recognize the fact that this licking stimulus is necessary for young animals.

The extraordinary story of the two children in India who were kidnaped and actually reared by a wolf, tells of how the older child, when brought back to civilization, acted like a wild creature and showed no signs of responsiveness to kindness until the missionary's wife, who was taking care of her, began to give her a regular daily massage. This was partly to correct the muscles of her hands and feet, distorted from traveling on all fours, and partly to find a method to give her some form of human contact. Almost immediately the child responded with signs of affection, and eventually, after this treatment, she learned to speak a few words and to adopt in some measure the ways of social life.

To the average mother, all too often, bathing and grooming are simply hygienic processes to be performed conscientiously and thoroughly. She does not recognize the fact that in these activities an important contribution is made to the child's sense of touch and to the response of his reflexes. Considering the neatness schedule is not enough. A true mother will recognize that her baby's bath is not only a cleansing process but something that is to him an experience in feeling which contributes greatly to his comfort and nervous well-being as well as to his awareness of his own body.

One mothering activity which is invariably overdone is that of diapering. Many mothers and nurses spend the better part of their time in attempting to keep the small baby dry. This is largely unnecessary in the first months, except for the comfort of the adults handling the child. For the infant himself it is usually a disadvantage because it focuses his developing attention on this part of the anatomy. Some mothers brag that they use as many as forty diapers a day "in order to teach the baby cleanlinesss right from the day of his birth." As a matter of fact, what they are doing is precisely the opposite. Unknowingly, they may teach the child to focus attention in this area, which should come through other avenues of stimulation, and they thus foster later emotional reactions which become deeply involved with the function of elimination. A healthy young baby, one to four months, unless he is cold or chafed, is not in the least disturbed by being wet, and six diapers a day are ample unless the child is ill. It is difficult for mothers to grasp the idea that the baby begins early to react to her activities and is not merely an eating or eliminating automaton.

Another type of sensation which is well developed at birth is the sense of body position—the kinesthetic, or muscle, sense. If a baby is placed on a flat surface so that the body is free to roll in any direction, he usually reacts with a startle and cries. (In a crib, the child sinks slightly into the mattress so that he feels a certain support.) If lifted suddenly or carried carelessly, the same reaction occurs. Some babies in our study group did not nurse because they were insecurely held; that is, the mother was either inexperienced and uneasy or she was indifferent to the child's comfort. Whereas, gentle movement, firm holding, frequent changes of body position, and rocking caused fretful infants to nurse contentedly. This primitive sense of position is extremely important in the development of a feeling of security in the infant.

From earliest times, devices have been created for the satisfaction in babies of the need for rhythmic movement, although for the most part the significance of the need was not known. Foremost among these devices, from the point of view both of time and of universality, stands the once-honored cradle. This quaint piece of furniture nicely takes the place of the rhythmic activity of the mother's uterus and the swaying movements of her body with which the child was familiar before birth. The cradle, therefore, has a sound biological basis when it is used judiciously. It is extremely unfortunate for the infant that it has been discarded to a large extent along with the comfortable rocking chair which used to be such an important item of furniture in any well-ordered nursery. Their disuse seems to be due to the inability of the adult to recognize when the infant is ready to substitute his own activities for passive rocking.

The Negro mammies of the old South, wise in their own intuition, held the newborn child in their arms or on their laps a great deal, rocking him gently to-and-fro with rhythmic regularity, often to the accompaniment of a soft monotonous song. They were unaware of the fact that this procedure served an important biological purpose, but they sensed intuitively that it resulted in the well-being of the baby. The few nurses of the old school who are left look with great contempt upon the stationary furniture of the modern nursery. However, as is the case with some parents today, they did not recognize the progressive stages of muscular development by which the baby gradually provides his own exercise, so that rocking gradually becomes unnecessary. The continuance of these comfortable activities beyond the appropriate time fosters passivity and dependence in the child, rather than the beginnings of self-dependence, which all good nurses and mothers must have constantly in mind.

Still another type of feeling well developed in the newborn baby is sensitivity to sound. The primal fear of sudden, loud noises has been noted by all observers of infants. The child reacts much as he does to an insecure body position, that is, with a startle. And here, it is the early stimulation of the human voice, preferably the mother's, which enters most deeply into listening and brings the deep reassurance the baby needs.

One way of dealing with the somewhat older child's introduction to sound survives in his toys—the squealing rubber devices, rattles, and bells, which amuse him after the third or fourth month—which play an important part in assisting him to adjust to varying degrees of noise.

Sensitivity to light does not require much attention. The baby, from birth, readily adjusts himself, for the pupil of the eye reacts to light immediately after birth, and, after the first few days of life, there is very little danger that the infant may get too much light stimulus, unless he is placed directly facing the sun. Babies in a darkened nursery are frequently seen gazing at windows, lamps, or light-colored walls, as if the stimulus were highly agreeable to them. When they have had enough, they close their eyes. Staring is a primary activity and should not be interfered with. The first true focusing of the eyes for any length of time occurs usually in connection with feeding, when the infant fixes his eyes first on the breast and later on the face of the mother.

Perhaps the most convincing evidence of the importance of rhythmical stimulation of tactile and muscle senses comes from the child who does not get, or who abruptly loses, appropriate maternal care. Under these circumstances, the child may react with various forms of automatic repetitive activity. Thumb-sucking, the best known and most obvious of these so-called habits, is discussed at length in another chapter. Head rolling, body rolling, and various other forms of hyperactivity, including masturbation, sometimes develop. In this way, natural behavior activities become exaggerated into troublesome habits.

An actual case will show the usual sequence. Baby Sally,

who was breast-fed and cared for only by her mother, developed well for the first four and a half months. At this time the mother was suddenly called away from home and the baby had to be weaned abruptly. The child was left in charge of an aunt who gave her the most conscientious care, exactly as it had been prescribed by a pediatrician. For fear that the infant would be handled too much, the aunt had been instructed not to pick her up; accordingly, she did not hold the baby for bottle feedings or fondle her. During the first week of the mother's absence no noteworthy reaction was observed. The child did not cry and apparently slept very soundly at night. However, a marked pallor developed in spite of scrupulous hygienic attention to fresh air, sunlight, and diet. By the end of the second week, the aunt was horrified to discover that when going to sleep, the child rolled her head violently, at times knocking it on the side of the crib. Not long after this, she began to bang her head with her fists during the day, at times picking at her hair. This behavior continued off and on for a period of two months. Finally, in desperation, the aunt decided that a psychiatrist must see the child, because she had the idea that some serious nervous disorder had developed. In the meantime, the mother had returned, and it was not difficult to outline a course of treatment, which she carried out in an excellent and even exaggerated fashion, so that the child rapidly recovered, soon being restored to an entirely normal condition. Breast-feedings were, of course, not resumed, but excellent mothering enabled this infant to overcome the results of the combination of sudden weaning from the breast and the loss of the mother's presence.

A vitally important element in an infant's feeling life—usually overlooked—is his sensuousness. After the major physiological adjustments following birth have been made, it becomes evident to any unprejudiced observer that the child who is well cared for is getting pleasure from his body and that he reacts with a warm glow of well-being in the dovetailing of his activities with those of his mother. Nature seems to have a purpose in this earliest biological endowment with pleasure, for it gives the child a sense of the goodness of his physical self. It puts the first stamp on the rightness of physical pleasure, which is one of the basic roads to happiness. The child's body is the tool which introduces him to life, and he must feel that it is a good tool. His mental SELF and his awareness develop hand in hand with the physical. With these facts in mind, it need not be alarming to parents to know that these early erotic feelings are the first expression of the mating instinct, which is also inborn equipment. Recent experiments of Harlow with monkeys, in which he substitutued a "dummy mother" of terry cloth, resulted later in the animal's refusal to mate. Erotic feeling is diffuse in a baby, but it is not misplaced and does not imply something evil which must be weeded out.

Erotic feeling is a kind of bonus of the senses which is a natural accompaniment of all growing activities. Somewhat later it becomes localized and organized in the genitals. It can serve to isolate the child or it can cement family relationships. The urge to deny or combat this feeling in a young child leads inevitably to a sense of guilt or anxiety and consequent resentment. Gentle and casual acceptance and tactful diversion when indicated pave the way to understanding and control.

When Freud first introduced the facts of infantile sexuality, an enormous storm of indignation and protest arose. The well-established ideas of "childhood innocence" tottered or were at least threatened. Yet those parents who are able to observe their children without anxiety and without the conviction that sex is a threatening evil in life, whose existence must be denied until adolescence, found that these reactions in the infant were obvious.

A four-months-old baby likes repetitive patting and stroking, he squirms and coos when he is kissed all over. His tiny fingers soon begin to explore his own body with evident satisfaction, wandering at times into the navel and genital regions. Baby boys are known to have erections from the time of birth. A one-year-old likes to be naked, to have admiring audiences when he is bathing and being dressed, he likes to snuggle in bed with parents. Tickling, if not too violent, causes laughter and excitement. All of these activities are natural and not a cause for concern, *unless they are overdone*. However, an excess of kissing and fondling can initiate a demand for these body pleasures and a later fixation on infantile forms of erotism. The difficulty lies in those parents who themselves are frustrated or lonely in their personal lives and get too much satisfaction from continuous or exaggerated fondling of the child. If they are not aware of the latent erotism of the infant they can easily overstimulate him, making him more demanding and creating tensions and anxiety.

Feeling, then, is as fundamental in the life of the young infant as is food. As with food, either starving or overfeeding causes harm. The part of the mother in all these delicate processes through which the infant feels his way outward is to hold out a helping hand at the moment when it is needed. She is the child's first and most important teacher, who gives him the fundamentals of his education in living. It is mothering, wise, tender, and mature, growing out of her fulfillment as a woman, which alone can make this subtle contribution to the infant's psychological growth.

7

Some Suggestions About Toilet Training

SO FAR, it has been pointed out in every chapter the importance of giving prompt help to a baby in his adjustment to the complicated process of living. However, in the matter of elimination, the opposite advice is needed, for natural elimination is a function which, from the beginning of life, may be disturbed by too early prompting. Here casualness must be cultivated, and whether we like it or not we must give Nature plenty of time to complete the development of the nerves and muscles which control evacuation. The reason is that certain primary feelings of the body and its control develop in close association with these functions, so, in order not to intrude on this self-regulation, we must set aside our fastidiousness for the time and let Nature do the prompting.

The general tendency has been for mothers and nurses to feel excessive urgency and responsibility in this area of child training, often neglecting other needs in the feverish attempt to "establish cleanliness." In regularizing this particular function of elimination, it is without question better to wait until the child can sit securely on a potty-chair with his feet on the floor and has command of a few signs or words with which to communicate his needs. It is surprising how early in life an infant develops an awareness of his gastrointestinal Self. His participation and readiness in matters of intake and output are a primary nucleus of cooperation and future behavior with parents and society, and his beginning mastery of these functions is important to other areas of self-control. Intensive study of large numbers of children and the various methods used in their training has shown psychologists that the character and personality of an individual are influenced deeply by the way in which his eating and eliminating functions were handled in the first year of life. Depending upon the stage of development of the baby when toilet training is begun and upon the sensitiveness of the individual child, the results in later life may be: a tremendous preoccupation with toilet functions; a feeling that others are intruding in private affairs; overcleanliness with compulsive ideas about bathing or else its opposite, persistent untidiness and refusal to wash. The emotional attitude of a mother or nurse who trains the baby too early, too suddenly, or too rigidly may bring about nervous tensions in the child and various forms of negative protest.

The great psychologist Sigmund Freud first pointed out the influence these primary functions and their control have on character formation. He found in the long and painstaking psychoanalytic study of many adults that the qualities of stubbornness, self-will, and stinginess may be regularly traced back to individual difficulty in early training to cleanliness.

"Shall I forget about the whole problem of toilet training for a year or two and turn the house into a laundry?" asks a young mother who has come for advice about the training of her baby. There are very few problems which forgetting has really helped, and certainly this is not one of them. During the baby's first months of life, parents may begin to observe the natural rhythm of his bowel movements and his reaction to this function which, even this early, begins to cause him excitement. In breast-fed babies, elimination, like most other bodily activities, is self-regulating, and a rhythm becomes established early if the mother is casual and does not show disgust and annoyance herself. Movements occur from three to five times a day, usually soon after nursing. The baby shows little reaction at this time. In the second or third month, a change comes about, and movements are fewer and firmer. The child shows some kind of excitement just before evacuation takes place. He may squirm as if he were about to cry, or he may seem to become very attentive. His limbs may stiffen out or draw up tightly. Breathing changes are noticeable, with either a very rapid respiration or a tendency to hold the breath. Babies of three to six months often fix the eyes on the mother with an expression of deep attention. As one mother said, "I thought my baby was beginning to know me because he looked at me so hard and seemed to smile." Then she continued with great disgust, "He was only getting ready to move his bowels." Babies sense very early that in these functions something of a very personal nature is happening which brings them a feeling of well-being and relieves disagreeable tension. Later it gives an important sense of personal accomplishment. This activity must not be interfered with because the first year of life is predominantly a biological rather than a cultural period, in which the nervous system is getting its most rapid growth and control. Hence the child cannot be called upon to adjust himself to outer conventionalities which may be more easily learned and accepted after the inner nervous organization is stabilized. Adjustments are better accomplished from within, with only wise aid from mother when distress is indicated.

One theory of toilet training, which is very much in vogue, advocates that as early as the second month of life the mother should hold the baby over a small potty in her lap several times a day and wait till "something happens." Often a soap suppository or even the little finger is introduced to get the idea across. This procedure works with apparent success with some infants, and a three-months' infant, by means of much determination and more manipulation, may be induced not to soil diapers. This relieves the laundry problem and gives a fastidious mother an inordinate feeling of pride in her own accomplishment and in the "cleanly instincts" of her child. However, his own early feeling of body control is thus negated and his primary sense of accomplishment is disturbed.

There are many other angles to be considered in this inappropriate procedure. In following the future development of several babies trained in this way so early in life, it was found that with any change of routine or with absence of the trainer the entire system broke down, and reestablishing it was an almost insuperable task, calling forth intense resistance of the small child and a long and difficult period of reestablishing control. A more serious angle to this early training procedure is the nervous tension arising in the child accompanied by feelings of protest, often by retention and constipation. A sense of mother's disappointment and disapproval may also initiate early feelings of guilt; breath holding may appear in the effort to control elimination, because the muscle of the diaphragm is involved in this control, so that later on an uncertainty of speech may become involved.

Children vary in getting control of elimination as in other areas of self-dependence, muscular control, and adaptation to family life. We found that the best general plan which brought the surest and most lasting results was to be observant but entirely permissive for the first year at least. When the child can speak or indicate what is going on inside him, he may be given the opportunity of the potty-chair once or twice a day, his feet securely on the floor and his hands grasping the arms of the seat. Many babies respond at once, but others require several months before they make the necessary association. The surest plan is to proceed slowly without tension. A child of one year already senses disappointment in parents. For this reason, the tolerance and self-control of the parent is of the greatest significance.

8

Life Rhythms and Artificial Schedules

ONE OF THE more subtle stories of ancient mythology is the tale of Procrustes, who shaped people to fit the beds, instead of supplying beds to fit people. This process of designing a mold to fit an average man and pouring all mankind into the mold is still being practiced, for its motivation is often a love of organization rather than a desire for progress. Assorted shapes and sizes in temperament and personality, even in children, seem to strike the businesslike person as untidy, and some reformers apparently dream of the day when we shall all think alike, feel alike, and look alike.

Many young mothers start out with a passion for standardization. It may be that they are hoping, very naturally and quite understandably, that once the baby gets going on a good schedule, he will be as dependable as train service and give his mother a chance to have some life of her own. In any case the importance of routine in the life of the infant has always been recognized, and he himself shows by his good response to regularity that he has indeed an inner need for outward system.

There is, however, considerable misconception as to the relationship between inborn natural rhythms of behavior and the artificial schedule of activity which may be imposed upon the child suddenly by the parents into whose hands he has been delivered. The average healthy baby is born with a fairly well-established natural rhythm of functional activity, which is often only temporarily disturbed by the process of birth. Yet, in spite of our knowledge to the contrary, we act as though the child does not begin to function until the moment he is born, and we forget that he is endowed by Nature with activities which have been in operation for many weeks. Any arbitrary attempts to set up and maintain an artificial schedule on any basis other than this spontaneous behavior, natural to the healthy baby, cannot but be disturbing to his development.

Routine for the young infant is not, then, as it is with the adult, simply a matter of convenience. It is, rather, to bring about proper exercise and balancing of a baby's body functions until the central nervous system is mature enough to take over its primary role of adapting. Actually, a child's routine might be called a primary learning process through which body activities, by means of repetition, become charged with functional energy. The mother, of course, is the loving teacher. In somewhat the same way that an adult learns to play the piano or acquire any other accomplishment—by constant repetition—so the baby "learns" the behavior which builds his body and shapes his personality—through regular repetition. Perhaps never again in his life does he have such a long list of study subjects! When this first routine is interrupted or when new experiences or even new foods are introduced before he is ready for them, his equilibrium and balance may be seriously disorganized. In the first weeks of life, it is necessary for the mother to give close attention to the routine which suits *her* baby, for no two babies are alike.

It is helpful to remember that the baby is doing his full share of the job of getting adjusted to the world. The extensive physiological changes going on within him at birth necessarily mean certain irregularities of behavior, and these cannot be organized suddenly. The coordination of vitally important functions must be prompted and directed by the mother, and after that the gradual establishment of a routine of general handling is not difficult, for as soon as these rhythms are well established according to inner law and given full exercise and satisfaction, the baby's development proceeds for a time on its own momentum. The more fully the mother can give herself to these first postnatal adjustments of the baby, the more ready both will be for the next stage, that of beginning independence. She will have taken the first step toward making the infant a self-maintaining individual. Who knows what time and trouble she may thus have saved herself ultimately!

Certain types of irregular behavior, recognizable after studying large groups of newborn infants, must be understood before they can be redirected. For example, many infants immediately after birth are excessively stuporous. Formerly we thought that they had been injured mechanically at birth. These babies need much more supervision than the more alert ones. This stupor may mean that the oxygen economy of the brain has been deeply disturbed either before or during birth and that the metabolism in the brain stem is inadequate to maintain breathing and other vital functions. This is probably not true sleep but a partial asphyxia. Extreme care must be taken in attempting to arouse these infants. They must be helped to breathe more adequately. This can be done best by stimulating them to suck, by tipping the head down to get more blood into the brain circulation, and by stroking the head and face. It is sometimes necessary to hold such an infant in the arms frequently in order to feel the tone of the muscles and watch the color of the skin, as well as the breathing movements.

In contrast to the stuporous type is the hyperactive infant who cries a great deal and gets too little rest. This child, as a rule, is also having difficulty with his oxygen supply, but his reflexes are somewhat better developed than are those of the stuporous child. His diaphragm, as well as his general body muscles, act to protect him and keep in circulation what oxygen he has. The prolonged crying which often accompanies his restlessness is commonly a spasmlike action of the diaphragm. The frantic body movements aid in dilating the capillaries of the lungs and in forcing more blood into the brain. These babies are often quieted simply by lowering the head and initiating sucking activity. It appears that the tension of the mouth and general body muscles alternates, and that shifting from one to the other activity is invaluable. Attempts made to restrain the restless movements of the child or to stop his crying by other means are unphysiological and usually make the condition worse.

Another type of unbalanced behavior is seen in the baby who sucks to excess. Some infants are born sucking the thumb or some of the fingers, and, occasionally, swollen and macerated thumbs of the newborn give evidence of finger-sucking before birth. This early sucking does not necessarily mean that the child is hungry for food, but that he needs this first mouth stimulation which assists him to breathe, increases the amount of blood sent to his brain, and relieves tension. Whether or not food hunger is present must be determined by observation and by accurate calculation of weight, food requirements, and actual food intake after the infant has been fed several times. Babies who suck vigorously in the first days of life are, as a rule, developing psychically at a rapid rate and are peculiarly sensitive. They can be helped by diverting a part of this tension from the mouth zone to the skin by the means of oil rubs, frequent bathing, and gentle massage. Unusual care must be given to their rest periods. Sudden loud noises should be avoided.

Any well-considered schedule must, then, of necessity take into account the balance of all the infant's native activities, and the daily routine must be carefully and gradually worked out with this in mind. To summarize: If the newborn infant sucks his thumb too much, this is the expression of oral tension, and the child's craving must be respected and attempts be made to gratify it appropriately. If he cries excessively, he may be overdoing a primitive form of breathing activity to protect himself from oxygen-want. If he is too stuporous, some of the rapidly developing brain tissues may suffer from not being oxygenated, and there is the danger that he may go into a state of inanition or slip back into ways in which he used to function before birth. Unless he gets help, the infant's organism must necessarily use any mechanisms at his disposal. Exaggerated or inappropriate use of one mechanism in place of another often means habit formation and subsequent behavior problems, for even in this early period of life, habits are formed rapidly and insidiously, and their prevention is distinctly easier than their cure.

The effect of interrupting the first routine is often seen when an infant is taken home from the maternity hospital. Several days of restlessness follow. Frequently physiological upsets occur, such as food regurgitation or loose stools, and still more frequently, there is exaggerated crying or other disturbance of breathing. The inexperienced mother cannot see that any actual change of routine has occurred because she follows conscientiously in general outline the methods for the care of the child which had been instituted in the hospital and in which she has been instructed. However, the extreme sensitivity of the infant to such factors as changes in temperature, light, or sound, handling by strange persons, slight differences in ventilation or in hardness or softness of the bed, is not usually appreciated. It is difficult for an adult to realize how distressing it may

be to the young infant to have to become adjusted to the
new world. One is reminded of seedlings that wilt on trans-
planting and must be specially tended and protected. We
find, for example, when a baby is placed in a room where
sudden loud noises can reach him, such as from a bus pass-
ing at frequent intervals, a doorbell ringing or a sudden
clatter of dishes, he reacts sharply to the sudden stimulation. On the other hand, our study showed that when infants were taken home from a hospital nursery where there
was more or less bustle of human sounds and where lights
were on and off, they gave an equally strong reaction to the
stillness of an entirely quiet room. As we have said, the
stimulation given a small baby has to be as carefully considered as his food intake, if the child is to be stable.

An elderly grandmother of one of the infants in our
study told the writer the following story, which illustrates
well what may happen when a radical interruption comes
into an infant's regulated routine, particularly when separation from the mother has occurred. The father of the
seven-weeks-old grandson was killed in an accident. As the
grandmother explained it, the "infant somehow knew" and
almost immediately began to wail violently, keeping up
this distressed crying fairly constantly for several days.
When the suggestion was made that some alteration in the
child's routine was responsible for the disturbance, she insisted that the child had been unusually well-cared for. A
trained nurse had been engaged to relieve the mother during this period and to make sure that the infant had the
usual attention. It never occurred to this good woman that

the introduction of a strange person, no matter how well trained, into the life routine of the infant may be an extremely serious matter. In addition to the factor of the new nurse, no one had observed that a constantly ringing doorbell was just outside the baby's room. When the household came back to normal, the string of visitors had stopped, and the nurse was dismissed, the mother again took over the care of her child and with a slight amount of help and advice was able to bring him back into functional equilibrium.

When a baby must remain over long periods in a hospital because of nutritional or other disorders, he often suffers because the nurse in charge is frequently changed in the course of the hospital routine. An infant who is convalescing nicely and thriving under the care of a familiar nurse may relapse or develop some new symptom following a change in personnel, even though the new nurse may be excellent in her care of the child.

An example from an actual case will show to what lengths a tiny human organism will go when a familiar relationship, which an adult might think far beyond a child's range or perception, is disturbed. Baby Sam was placed immediately after birth in the care of a most capable and motherly trained nurse because the mother was a professional woman and did not want to interrupt her business any longer than was necessary. This child appeared perfect in every respect and his routine care was carried out with ease and the greatest precision. Development proceeded smoothly. When the child was five months old, the nurse was called away suddenly by a death in her family. The mother, without realizing the significance of the relationship between the nurse and the child and hoping to have the old nurse return after a short time, took care of the baby herself. She was not at all a novice in these matters. Yet, although she had had several years of nursing experience in an excellent infant's hospital, she had never taken care of her own child, so that she was a stranger to him. Her surprise was great, then, when her seemingly normal baby absolutely refused to take food. For twenty-four hours, the mother, the father, and other members of the family worked in shifts attempting to give this baby a bottle, but without success. Eventually, the child went into a stuporous state and seemed to be sleeping most of the time. A pediatrician was called in consultation and after the most careful examination could find nothing wrong with the infant. The "hunger strike" persisted, however, and food was finally introduced artificially through a stomach tube. In desperation, the mother telegraphed the old nurse that she must come back to save the baby's life. Fortunately, the nurse was able to return, and within a few days the old routine was restored.

Following this episode, the nurse was closely questioned as to her handling of the child. The parents found that she had given the infant the additional gratification of being held in her arms, fondled, or sung to while taking his bottle, so that the satisfaction of her presence had assumed exaggerated prominence. The sight and sound stimulus of the familiar nurse connected with the feeding was necessary for the function to go on smoothly. It is interesting that this child, whose history has been followed carefully for four years, reacts to any privation or disappointment by refusing to eat. Displays of temper or other outbursts are rarely seen in him, and he is in other respects a passive and docile child. An outstanding feature in his development has been a persistent refusal to chew solid foods. He was beginning to teethe at the time when he was first deprived of his nurse and an association was built up, or, in the terms of the school of Pavlov, the child was "conditioned" against chewing. Such a sudden early change of nurses can be a serious matter against which definite precautions must be taken. The result in the developing mental life of the child is much more distrubing than a complete change in food. In fact, in cases where the mother or the familiar nurse remains with the child and gives him consistent care, the food can be changed with less serious result.

In planning the life routine of the baby from birth to speech period, perhaps the most important factor to be considered is the element of continuity. Sudden changes, as we have seen, exert an extremely disorganizing influence on nervous integration. This is particularly true in the first three months of life, but continues to be of significance until after the speech period has begun. When the baby has reached this stage, disorganization does not come about so readily.

Such a drastic change as sudden weaning in the first three months inevitably brings about serious consequences. New activities, new foods, or new persons can be tolerated only when the mother or nurse is a constant and unchanging factor. Mothers who are engaged in business or in the arts often have a feeling that they would like to give the baby the benefit of breast-feeding for two or three months before returning to their outside occupation. This idea on the part of a mother implies that she thinks only of the nutritional aspect of the feeding and not of the contact experience and the developing of a relationship. If a mother must return to work a few months after the birth of the child, it is a better plan to start the infant with some bottle feeding which can be continued without change while the child is on a predominantly milk diet.

Another important consideration is: Who shall have the chief care of the child during this prespeech period? When an outside nurse is employed, it is vitally important to engage one who will agree to remain through at least this period.

The amount of attention, with its resulting stimulation, which the child is to receive from various members of the family has to be considered and regulated. After the third month a short social period can be arranged safely, morning and afternoon, but always at regular intervals, when members of the immediate family who are experienced can hold the child or take over some part of the care. However, irregular visiting and the sudden picking up of a small infant is disturbing and under no circumstances should they be allowed. One mother is enough, provided she really mothers.

A tentative suggestion follows for the routine of a baby from one to four months. This is in no sense applicable to all babies and would have to be modified to suit the needs of an individual child. It is also to be clearly understood that the schedule which follows is not concerned with the food hunger of infants, which in modern practice is usually met adequately enough, but with the problem of meeting an infant's equally deep hunger for stimulation. It is simply a schematic arrangement which brings into perspective the rhythmical needs of the infant. Please remember always that *time,* for the young baby, is the rhythm of his inner needs.

THREE-HOUR BEHAVIOR INTERVAL

FIRST THREE MONTHS

1. *When the baby spontaneously wakes* (6–6:30 A.M.)
Take up from bed, hold in lap for a few minutes, and rock gently, while stroking the head (Personal need)
Sucking period, 20–30 minutes. Food hunger predominates at this time (Sucking need)
Diapering. The average baby has a bowl movement about one-half hour after this first morning activity (Elimination)
7–8:30. Quiet in bed (Sleep)

2. *When the baby becomes restless* (8:30–9 A.M.)
Complete bath with fresh clothing. Allow 5 to 10 minutes of completely free random movement without clothing before bath, in a very warm room. After one month
Sucking period, 20 minutes
Fresh diaper
9:30–11:30. Quiet in bed. This is the ideal time to observe

the regularity and depth of the child's breathing. The pink color during sleep and the relaxation of muscle tone indicate that the baby is getting enough stimulation and is breathing adequately. Allow the baby to rouse spontaneously and cry for several minutes before the next period of mothering activity. This is a good breathing exercise. But here a word of caution is necessary. The mother must distinguish between crying which is done as a breathing exercise and crying which denotes a need on the part of the infant for his accustomed mothering or some painful stimulus. In general, we might say that a young child should not be left to cry, but, upon crying, should receive the judicious mothering activities which his needs demand.

3. *Noon time* (12 M.–1. P.M.)
   Take up and hold baby in lap, gently stroking head
   Sucking, ad lib (30 minutes is average)
   Fresh diaper
   1–3. Quiet in bed. Ideal time for sun bath and fresh (not cold) air

4. *Afternoon rousing-up period* (3–3:30 P.M.)
   Take up and hold in lap. Gentle moving about, 15 minutes
   Sucking period, 20–30 minutes
   Fresh diaper. Bowel movement often takes place at this time
   4–5:30. Quiet in bed

5. *Evening* (5:30 P.M. This period later becomes visiting hour)
   Take up and hold in lap. Gentle moving about or rocking.
Full bath or sponging. Dress for the night
   Sucking, 20–30 minutes
   Fresh diaper
   Rock and sing to sleep (Emphasis on stimulus intake)
   7–10. Quiet in bed

6. *Take up for feeding* (10 P.M. or when baby awakens spontaneously)

Sucking, ad lib. Gentle stroking of head

Fresh diaper

Quiet in bed until spontaneous restlessness or crying occurs, usually 2 or 3 A.M. until past three months

7. *Night feeding* (2–3 A.M.)

Usually during the fourth month the baby, after his 10 P.M. feeding, begins to sleep through the night.

Note: For the child's best welfare, diapering should be done after the feeding period, for this on the average is the usual time for elimination to take place. Because of the individual differences in babies, it is unwise during the first months of a child's life to be rigid in regard to standardizing schedules. As has been emphasized, importance must be laid on the study of the spontaneous activity of the individual baby; on observing his times of awakening; on the intervals at which restlessness tends to occur; on sucking needs; on stimulus needs; on the average time of day when bowel movements tend to occur; and on frequency of urination. On the basis of these observations a schedule may gradually be laid down.

FOUR-HOUR BEHAVIOR INTERVAL

ROUTINE AT FOUR MONTHS

Evidences of mental activity are now clearly seen. Vocalizing and teething become prominent after this time.

1. *When the baby spontaneously wakes* (6–6:30 A.M.)

Take up from bed, hold in lap for a few minutes, and rock gently while stroking the head

Sucking period, 20–30 minutes. Food hunger predominates at this time

Diapering. The average baby has a bowel movement after this first morning activity

7–9. Well-integrated baby lies quietly and plays with fingers, vocalizes, or sleeps again

2. *Bath period. When baby becomes restless* (9–10 A.M.)

Free exercise without clothing in a very warm room, 10 minutes. Complete bath and fresh clothing

Sucking period, 20–30 minutes

Fresh diaper

10–1. Nap. Wait for spontaneous awakening. This is true sleep in which there should be complete muscle relaxation. (By this time the breathing rhythm should be well established so that no further close observation is necessary unless the child has been ill

3. *Lunch period* (1:30–2 P.M.) Take up from bed and hold in lap 20 minutes

2 o'clock. Sucking period. Following this, *time to initiate chewing activity.* Cracker or toast placed in the mouth for jaw exercise 5 to 10 minutes after sucking

2:45. Fresh diaper. Sleeping in fresh air or sun bath out in carriage

4. *Social period.* (5:30 P.M.) Emphasis on stimulus hunger

Visiting hour, preferably for father

6 o'clock. Sucking, followed by singing and rocking to sleep

Fresh diaper

7–10. Sleep

5. *Take up for feeding* (10 P.M.)

Move about. Last meal

Fresh diaper

The average four-months' baby will sleep approximately from 11 to 6

Note: Only insofar as the mother or nurse is able to recognize and work with the natural activities of the infant will development proceed smoothly, both in the more strictly physiological processes of eating, breathing, and sleeping and in the feeling experiences which lead to the beginning of mental functioning. To the casual observer, the spontaneous activities of the individual baby may seem to have little meaning or may not seem to be best for the welfare of the developing child. They have, however, a deep biological sense, as we have seen, and must be respected for both the physical and the mental health of the child. The gradual direction of these activities into regular and more appropriate channels is the sum and substance of the business of early mothering. Observations of elimination in the next four months give a basis on which to build subsequent training to cleanliness. No attempts at training of bowel control can be made advantageously until after the child can sit steadily without support and until definite vocalizing has begun.

9

Babies Must Not Be Thwarted

"CHILD PRECIOUS above all!" prays the Mexican midwife after the baby's first bath, "Ometecuhtli and Omecihuatl have created you in the twelfth heaven, in order that you should be born into this world. Know, then, that this world is sorrowful, full of pain, troublesome and solitary; it is a vale of tears; and that you, when an adult, must eat your bread with pain and earn it by your hands." *

All too many modern parents seem to be motivated by this ancient philosophy, grimly training their babies to prepare for the worst before they have made the first adjustments to life. As a matter of fact, Nature is quite aware of what she is about when she gives the child his instincts. The chaotic behavior of the newborn infant has a sense, and any restricting of his natural ways at an early age may very well endanger the maturing of delicate mechanisms that make it possible for the small body to live and breathe and have its being. Thwarted in one direction, the infant will take other ways to express himself and relieve tension,

* Heinrich H. Ploss, *Das Kind in Brauch und Sitte der Völker* (3d ed., Leipzig, Th. Grieben, 1911).

developing protective habits that can distort normal growth, just as a plant that is kept from the light will adopt another way of getting what it needs, twisted and distorted though that way may be.

Most of the habits of infancy which parents think of as troublesome (thumb-sucking, crying at night, general restlessness, refusal to sleep) are useful activities which are not yet organized, and so, through a "bad habit," the baby is getting something vitally needed, but in an inappropriate way. Sometimes such habits represent behavior borrowed from another level of development, but usually they are a roundabout means of protection.

The human infant in the first months of life should not have to be restricted, for this causes exaggerated tension. If the effects of such experiences are not skillfully counteracted, behavior disorders may result. For the baby, the pleasure principle must predominate, and what we can safely do is gradually to bring order into his functions and make them easy and satisfying. Only after a considerable degree of maturity has been reached can we train an infant to adapt to the routine of a world outside of himself.

The antithesis to the idea of making life pleasant to the baby is found in the theory of making him sturdy by toughening him, letting him wait for food, reducing the danger of colds by cool baths, inappropriate clothing in cold weather, and by sleep in a cold bedroom. This is an obvious fallacy. These experiences, which may be stimulating to the adult, are damaging to an infant under one year of age. His metabolism is becoming stabilized to maintain body heat and at the same time to provide for growth and body activity and, most important of all, for completion of brain development. Such irregular and unnecessary experiences are a severe strain, requiring an adjustment of the circulation not easily made by a young infant. Inner developmental processes are going on at such a tremendous rate in the beginning of life that even with no unusual demands the resources of the small organism are taxed to the limit.

Of course, it is true that there is a subtle danger connected with the pleasure principle, in that it may become associated with one function at the expense of others. The pleasure of sucking, as we know, may easily become all absorbing. But this difficulty can be forestalled by providing other satisfying experiences (of body movement, of sound, or of rocking) which give a sense of well-being and relieve tension.

The word "thwarted" is used regardless of whether the thwarting is intentional on the part of the mother or is an inadvertent lack of warmth and attention. It may consist merely in neglecting to bring any of the primary body functions into action. To the infant who is characteristically passive and helpless it is all the same, in the first three months.

We have seen in a previous chapter some of the difficulty arising when the impulse to suck is not strong at birth and the mother neglects to help the infant make the process easy. A very young or weak child may not only tend to lose the ability to suck, but his entire motor system may lose its tone. He becomes stuporous and lethargic, his breathing irregular, and a marked pallor develops. This reaction, which in all probability is the basis of what has been called shock in infants, means that a general functional failure has taken place. Sometimes it is mistaken for food hunger. It may rarely occur in an older, better organized baby when he is suddenly separated from the mother, but the reaction is characteristic of the first three months. It shows dramatically the far-reaching effects of neglect of or interference with some basic functional drive.

Sometimes, instead of losing the sucking reflex, the child's mouth activity appears to become reversed; the reaction to his sucking difficulty is to push the nipple out of his mouth vigorously with his tongue. Along with this unusual tongue action, an exaggerated tone or tension develops in the body muscles, so that the small torso tends to arch backwards. It is interesting to note that premature babies fed artificially with a dropper very often show this reaction, but as soon as they are able to suck vigorously and frequently, rigidity begins to disappear. (This "extensor reaction" probably allows more spinal fluid and more blood to reach the brain.) Such a condition of tension must not be ignored. A similar rigid posture is seen in older children in pathological conditions such as meningitis, where there is pressure on the brain which deprives it of its blood supply.

The frustration reactions described in the preceding paragraphs apply mostly to infants of a sensitive type or to young or premature babies. The tendency of the more vigorous infant of three or four months is toward exaggerated sucking activity when he is not getting enough mouth stimulation. This often appears in the form of thumb-sucking. Sometimes this habit develops when the infant takes food too fast and does not exercise his mouth sufficiently or when he is fed concentrated food at infrequent intervals. Infants cannot be required to wait for their feeding, and they cannot be deprived of this fundamental activity of sucking or be unduly interrupted in its performance.

The main thing to remember is that thwarting must be looked upon not as a cure for early habits but all too often as a provocation of them. It is therefore a harmful practice for nurses to remove baby's hands from his mouth and to bind down his arms so as to make thumb-sucking impossible. Any restriction of movement can be harmful, as are attempts to stop excess crying other than by walking about, stroking, or singing.

The relationship between thwarting and habit formation is brought home in the somewhat unusual case of Baby Joe. His mother, a successful teacher in a private kindergarten, developed early in her pregnancy apprehension that either she or the baby would die at the time of delivery. In addition to this, she had a great dread of having to handle a newborn baby and felt sure that she would let him fall. She did not plan to nurse the coming infant and made no preparations for him. His clothing and crib were purchased by her sister at the last minute. It is interesting that this mother made quite a ritual of reading every book that she could find on the care of babies, picking out particularly those sections which advised against handling and spoiling the child. It was found later that, unknown to herself, she had a phobia for small infants.

Her baby, immediately at the birth, showed an intense need for stimulation. He sucked his thumb on the delivery table and had two or three fingers almost constantly in his mouth. He also sucked on his lower lip and later on even sucked his tongue. When placed at the breast for the first time, he was unable to grasp the nipple because the mother's breasts were small and undeveloped. He had to be taught to nurse through a nipple shield, which was a difficult procedure for him.

The mother was so uneasy that she seemed unable even to hold the child in a comfortable position where he might nurse adequately. Since he was thin and undernourished, he was given supplementary feedings from a bottle after each nursing. The child did not thrive during a two weeks' stay in the hospital after delivery and failed to gain the usual weight. But when he went home and the mother's sister, who had made all the preparations for his advent, took over his care, an immediate and dramatic change occurred. He responded so promptly to the soothing and comfortable care of this motherly woman that in a week's time he had put on several ounces of weight and appeared to be a normal and contented infant. He continued, however, to suck his fingers.

Shortly after this the kindly aunt had to return home to her own children, and the baby's mother, as awkward as before, undertook the care of her child, feeling that she had now "learned how" to do this. This unfortunate woman had had serious emotional difficulties in childhood due to intense sibling jealousy of a brother born when she was two. This had left her with a suppressed hostility to young infants. She could not cope with her child's need for mothering. She tried to stop the finger-sucking by binding the infant's arms to his sides with bandages. A few days later an emergency call to the hospital was made by the visiting nurse, who had discovered the child in a critical condition. When she had attempted to give him his bottle feeding, he could not hold the nipple with his lips. He was extremely pale, and his respiration was so rapid and shallow that she feared pneumonia. Rushed to the hospital, he was found to have no symptoms of infection, but was in a state of shock. He responded very well to treatment and within twenty-four hours was taken home again. Complete body massage twice a day was prescribed, more frequent and dilute bottle feedings were given (every three hours instead of every four), and the mother was encouraged to hold the child on her lap or to walk him about before and after each feeding. In this way he obtained the needed mothering stimulation. The acute condition of functional failure which proved to have resulted from unwonted neglect and from prohibition of finger-sucking, simultaneously with the loss of the motherly aunt, was soon relieved.

However, this mother again became the victim of her fears and could not handle the child. Baby Joe developed one form of disorganized behavior after another. At first there were attacks of hiccups for which no cause could be found. Severe constipation followed later, and at the age of two months another curious symptom appeared: he began to bleed from the navel. It seemed that this baby was functioning again as he had before birth and that the prenatal type of circulation had never been entirely abandoned. When this bleeding occurred, the mother, who had gotten a baby-sitter and gone back to her position as teacher, gave up those duties in order to concentrate once more on the care of her own child, who was now in a very critical condition. The baby improved slowly for a number of weeks and, with a great deal of help from a visiting nurse, appeared to have recovered.

This child was studied carefully by our visiting nurse through the first three years of his life. According to the record she made, he reacted to any change in routine or to the absence of his mother with severe respiratory symptoms resembling asthma, sometimes awaking from sleep with an attack of croup. Later he had periods of breath holding, frequent prolonged spells of hiccups, and on several occasions such violent crying that he became blue in the face and momentarily unconscious. These symptoms were always definitely related to some inattention or absence of the mother. She invariably reacted by giving the child an extra amount of attention, and this usually restored functional equilibrium.

Another case of striking functional disorganization following sucking difficulty, or thwarting, was that of Baby Sue. The first child of healthy, vigorous, middle-class parents, she was born without difficulty, was well nourished, and cried immediately at birth. On physical examination, she was found to be in perfect condition. Two factors contributed to her sucking difficulty: the most obvious was that the mother had slightly retracted nipples; the more subtle element in the frustration of the infant lay in the emotional attitude of the mother to nursing. She did not want to nurse the child and planned to return to her job as cook in a restaurant. However, a hospital nurse persuaded her to change her decision and to breast-feed her child.

The nurse in charge believed that such a vigorous infant needed no assistance in drawing out the nipples and stimulating breast secretion, and so the nipple shield, which is customarily used in such cases to give the infant more of a hold, was omitted. When placed at the breast, the baby displayed vigorous mouthing activity. Her head pushed forward and rotated itself in the so-called "seeking reflex." However it was impossible for her to make the necessary coordination with the lips, tongue, and hard palate to grasp the nipple. The mother, who having made her decision now felt that her maternal integrity depended on her nursing the child successfully, became highly excited and manipulated her breasts in an attempt to draw out the nipples. From this she had a severe inflammation which finally resulted in an abscess that precluded nursing.

Meanwhile, the baby, after a number of unsuccessful attempts, had stopped sucking and when placed at the breast became stuporous. If a rubber nipple were placed in her mouth, it was pushed out vigorously by the tongue. Her

head arched back stiffly, finally her entire body bent backward as if in protest, and her breathing became extremely
irregular. It looked as if she were vigorously resisting food.
In this position she swallowed large amounts of air and her
stomach became enormously distended. She had to be
placed on bottle feedings with a freely flowing nipple, because there was little sucking activity and the fluid simply
drizzled down her throat. It took approximately one hour
for the nurse to give her the three ounces of formula from
the bottle.

This baby became an air swallower, which frequently
caused her to regurgitate the food given with such difficulty. Her breathing was inadequate and the rigid posture,
with general tendency toward backward extension, continued even during sleep.

Through the painstaking efforts of the mother over
many days, a great deal of fondling and much stimulation
of the mouth with a nipple, the sucking reflex returned,
and a certain degree of organization was again established
in the child's functions. Sucking then became so exaggerated that it was almost continuous, and frequently the
baby pulled the bottle so far into her mouth that she would
gag or choke.

Then, once again, the child was thwarted. To check the
thumb-sucking which had become a constant activity, the
mother pinned the baby's sleeves to her clothing. The result was that the child again gradually became stuporous,
breathed very irregularly, swallowed a great deal of air,
and refused to take milk. When it was introduced by force,

she immediately vomited. By the end of the second month, she was in such a poor state of nutrition that she had to be placed in an infants' hospital, where the physicians in charge were convinced that she was suffering from either a brain injury or a constriction of the opening between the stomach and the intestines known as pyloric stenosis. Careful study, however, showed that she had neither of these maladies.

The infant was put on a diet of thickened cereal every two hours. This treatment proved highly successful, probably because the baby had an excess of attention with this rather difficult form of feeding and also because her mouth again had the stimulation it needed. Gradually the muscle tone of the stomach recovered, so that the air swallowed could be easily regurgitated without loss of food. On the advice of the physician, the baby was allowed to suck as much as she would, and no vomiting followed. After two weeks of painstaking care, her functions became reorganized and she returned home in good condition.

This child reacted normally as long as her mouth activity was not in any way interrupted and as long as she received adequate mothering. A short absence from her mother, however, resulted again in complete disorganization of function and put her in a state of extreme restlessness and anxiety.

This case was unusual and spectacular, but varying degrees of this same sort of difficulty were seen in any number of infants. Babies who are not immediately assisted in establishing this fundamental activity are thereby thwarted and suffer a loss of sensitivity. In addition to this, their breathing and gastrointestinal functions become disturbed. To redirect these basic body functions is not an easy matter.

It is clear, then, that apparently trivial frustrations or neglect of fundamental activities have a far-reaching effect on the physiological and beginning psychological organization.

The reaction of young babies to thwarting of early instinctual impulses varies, of course, with the constitution of each individual. Some infants develop crying habits; others, exaggerated sucking; a few, as we have seen, go into states of general functional failure, inanition, shock, or of hypertension.

The common belief of parents is that a young infant who is not getting something he needs vitally reacts immediately by crying, kicking, or other familiar forms of protest. This is usually true of babies past the third month of life who have not been ill and who have not suffered early emotional neglect, but it does not apply in the first weeks of life, particularly, to those who are somewhat premature or who have definitely shown signs of asphyxia after birth. These infants react in a much more subtle and indirect way to thwarting, by withdrawing or becoming negative. Their functional impulses in the first weeks are very diffuse. Their inner needs may be adjusted for some time by kicking, squirming, and crying, which tend to help circulation and better distribute the food supplies stored in the body tissues. But the obvious danger of this use of

inner reserves is that the supply may give out before mechanisms of intake become well enough developed for emergency requirements. In following the subsequent behavior
of children who suffered early oral frustration, it was
found that if definite efforts are not made immediately to
remedy the disturbance, serious consequences result, both
in the subsequent reactions of the child toward food and in
the emotional attitude toward the mother. Naturally, both
types of reaction have a special significance for the child's
mental or personality development. The prompt and adequate satisfaction of an infant's needs therefore not only is
of moment in his immediate welfare but is also vital in the
future adaptive development of a good personality and
successful relationships.

Crying habits develop in much the same way as sucking
habits. Crying of the infant in the first weeks of life is
breathing exercise. It becomes a habit when the child is
not comforted. The infant should be helped to develop
and get control of the mechanisms of respiration. He must
have adequate stimulation to keep the breathing center in
tone, in order that his breathing muscles may get the
proper exercise.

Additional insight into the development of all these
habits can be gained from a visit to a large home for found-
lings or to an institution where small children are
grouped together over long periods without considerable
individual care. One sees them in all sorts of odd postures,
many of them making rhythmic movements, such as
rolling the body, sticking one leg or arm through the bars

of the crib and waving it persistently, rolling the head or knocking it on the crib, and sometimes grimacing constantly. They also make odd sounds which are repetitive and mechanical. Nearly all are slow in speaking. On the other hand, some of them are completely lethargic and lie limply in bed, their large eyes wandering around as if they were in search of something.

But it must be remembered that these habits are not peculiar to institutions but often occur in homes where there is every comfort for the child, except emotional satisfaction which comes from mother love.

To find the meaning of this bizarre behavior has not been an easy task. Until its development had been observed from the beginning in a number of babies who previously had behaved normally, its origin remained unclear.

Close study of a number of such cases of children who were abandoned, or from whom maternal love was withdrawn for some more subtle reason, shows definitely that each child deprived of personal care must get for himself a substitute stimulation. The way in which he gets it depends on two factors—his individual constitution and the particular stage of development in which he happens to be when he suffers either early stimulus hunger or later emotional need. Autoerotic activity is found most consistently: some babies develop the habit of staring at lights or even at the sun; others, who are somewhat older and just beginning to vocalize, develop the habit of making rhythmic noises or humming; still older children, who are learning to talk, repeat words persistently and make rhymes. Invariably the

child who is deprived of individual mothering shows dis-
ordered behavior, together with a dulling of general
alertness.

On the other hand, when the mother-child relationship
is wholesome, normal behavior development proceeds so
smoothly and is so well integrated that it is difficult to see
the delicate interpersonal factors involved. It is from the
strange behavior of unmothered children that we gain one
of the best clues to the meaning of the early dependency
relationship, as well as an understanding of what early
"habits" mean.

10

Fathers

so MUCH has been said about the mothering of an infant, it might well be inferred that the role of the father in the early life of his child is negligible. Because this role may have to be an indirect one, it is even ignored at times, and this is one of the glaring defects of our modern system of child care. The lack of a father relationship early in life can leave a painful gap in a child's feelings. One of the most important impressions of an infant, even in his early months, is the experience that there are two sorts of people in the world quite different in quality, and appearance, but mutually complementary. This piece of awareness, which is introduced by parents, as a rule quite unknowingly, by the mere fact of their presence, has an unbelievably great effect in the child's later life and thinking. Two parents who have achieved maturity and happiness in their respective biological roles are the native right of every child. Hence, after the first weeks a pair of strong but gentle arms, a new smell, and new textures begin to register with the child. As time goes on, this first masculine experience takes shape and gets new meaning. An hour morning and night contributes immeasurably to the child's well-being and lessens considerably the chance of an exaggerated mother attachment. Two personal relationships are developing and both are good, and for the parents, this brings a new phase of maturity into the marriage. It is a shared project of creativeness, a new venture which is beneficial and contributes to their own emotional growth.

The average business or professional man today, unless he considers the matter well, may have very little regular time to devote to his infant. Yet if it is possible to arrange a daily period when he can observe and care for his baby, it is the ideal situation for both and contributes in a subtle and important way to the child's feeling of security. It gives a man a vital experience with the first principles of life which he can ill afford to miss.

Our modern setup for the care of pregnancy, birth, and early babyhood has so far taken the emotional factors of marriage very little into consideration. A great deal of attention is lavished on the mother by the obstetrician or the clinic she attends, and this is as it should be. However, it is a fallacy to consider the pregnant woman apart from her husband. Fortunately, the practice is becoming common of establishing clubs for fathers-to-be or at least of giving evening lectures for fathers with practical demonstrations of baby care. It is strange that such vital information as how to care for a baby and his needs in the first months has never become a universal part of the education of young people.

When there are serious and persistent maladjustments between parents, the child's psychological stability is inevitably threatened, and his development does not proceed smoothly. The youngest baby is affected from the beginning by the emotional tone in the parental relationship. However much both parents may know about infant psychology and however strongly they desire and intend to give their baby a good start in life, the tensions in the relationship are communicable to the child.

Young fathers-to-be frequently experience a deep emotional disturbance when the wife becomes pregnant. Sometimes they feel neglected and angry. Otherwise they lunge into new activities and seek the company of other men. This is a puzzling and humiliating matter to any man. He may suddenly discover in himself a repugnance to pregnant women and to young children. Also, when the baby is born he often senses a disturbing repugnance to the child and avoids contact with him. One reason for this is that fatherhood relates to experiences in a man's early life, such as sibling rivalry. As a child, he may have been emotionally shocked by the advent of a baby brother or sister for whom he was not prepared. The sudden appearance of the newcomer, without adequate explanation, indicates that his place has been taken away. At this age a child is unable to reason out the fact that there is enough affection for him, as well as for the newcomer. Small children *feel;* they do not think. The effect of this early emotional disturbance is often retained in adult life, although the individual is usually unaware that such feelings are part of his emotional make-up. Then, when the situation of his own fatherhood is upon him he reacts with panic, without recognizing the cause. This is a matter of great importance to

young married men and one which should be well understood.

Little Tom, for example, was brought to our group by
his mother when he was six years old. He was an inveterate
thumb-sucker and though he went willingly to school, he
showed no interest in learning or in playing with other children. His teacher reported to the mother that he kept his
thumb in his mouth most of the time. If she asked him a
question, he would answer with part of a sentence, would
then return his thumb to his mouth, and when she called
his name he would complete the answer. Obviously, the
other children in the class snickered and made fun of
Tom, which made him sad, but he continued to be absorbed in his own fantasies.

In conversation with the mother, she finally related that
there had been tension between herself and her husband
even before the birth of the little boy. Since his birth, the
father, a successful artist, had absented himself throughout
the day and most of the evening, becoming overly absorbed in his work. He insisted that a small child was entirely his mother's problem. (He himself was an only child.)
Tom's mother, in consequence, felt herself neglected and
became deeply resentful to both father and child. Although
she had determined to nurse Tom for at least four months,
she found this increasingly difficult, so after six weeks he
was abruptly put on bottle feedings. Following this, the
baby "waked every night at two o'clock and cried for
hours." This produced more tension in the parents and
overt resentment toward the little boy. When solid foods

were introduced into his routine, he had to be coaxed to eat and preferred to suck his thumb. However, when he was a year old, he would be seen to eat when no one was watching, so that his general physical health appeared to be good. The pediatrician was mystified as to why the parents made so many complaints about the child.

Tom resisted toilet training in the same way that he had refused to eat, until after he was four years old, and was still often incontinent at school age. He was on exceptionally bad terms with his mother and used to beg his father to allow him to sit in the studio and draw pictures.

The speech development of this little boy was decidedly delayed, and he still spoke with a lisp up to the time he went to school. He played very little with other children because they laughed at him.

A sister was born when Tom was two years old, and at this time his mother admitted frankly that she turned from him and his troublesome habits to the second child, a girl. As a result the sucking became intensified and continued in spite of all attempts to tie down his hands at night and to put bad-tasting chemicals on his fingers. The child, like an infant, turned to himself for comfort.

The mother's explanation of Tom's trouble was an interesting and frequent type of rationalization. She said that it had finally dawned on her that her husband's mother (whom she disliked intensely) had been in a mental hospital at the time that they were married and that the same mother-in-law had taken care of Tom at the time that his sister was born. She was quite convinced that heredity was the cause of the entire difficulty. With deep-seated anger, she remarked "You know, of course, the saying that you should drown the first one."

Fortunately Tom's father had become interested in him as he passed out of the baby stage. He agreed to have some hours of psychotherapy for himself in order to help the little boy. As a result, after three months he and Tom became buddies. They played ball together and little by little played games with the neighboring children. Tom was frequently allowed to sit with his father while he worked and to draw pictures. His thumb-sucking had entirely disappeared at the end of the year, and his progress through the first grade went on without further difficulty. Also some improvement in the marriage relationship came about by means of the insight these two fine parents gained into the causes of Tom's and their own emotions.

It is frequently said of a man who makes a phenomenal success in a difficult undertaking that some woman is the power behind the throne. Certainly, in a woman's greatest creative venture, the giving of life to a new human being and guiding him emotionally through infancy, her husband is the supporting power, but the success of the joint undertaking depends on the constancy of both.

I I

Early Emotional Development

THE RIGHTS of a baby to guidance in the development of his emotional life must be emphasized after the fourth month of life. He begins at this time to show, in addition to physical growth and health, the first specific emotional responses to his mother. His eyes focus for an appreciable time on her face, and he smiles in response to her presence, his entire motor system gradually becoming tense with excitement and anticipation. If she disappears too suddenly or if she is with him too little, he definitely cries for her. He has begun to develop awareness of his mother as an entity or person, on whom all his life's experiences are centered. She has become more than a comforting touch, the stimulus to his breathing, and the source of his food; she is now the "open-sesame" for strong new feelings of well-being and satisfaction or else of tension and disappointment.

This new emotional awareness of his mother is in the nature of a craving for her, but it is now definitely related to seeing and hearing, as well as to being moved about and to actual physical contact. The rapid development of eyes and ears, the so-called "distance receptors," is in progress and is becoming a pleasurable experience. The fourth month is a crucial period in early emotional development. From this time on, a new emphasis comes into mothering —and also fathering—for the development of the subsequent relational life. If the father has made a place for himself in the infant's experiences, this emotional period is shared, hence much simplified.

The feelings of the baby center predominantly in himself. It is through the mother that an infant gets his first feelings of what other human beings are like and he, in turn, begins to react to them with like or dislike. Love and hate are probably selective impulses implanted by heredity in certain areas of the brain, but the intensity of each emotion depends a great deal on primary experience. Careful nurture of positive emotion has a fundamental influence on subsequent training. The unloved child comes to feel that his parents are thwarting creatures who are necessary but obnoxious and to be defied. In time he will find that he has to adjust to them, but this adjustment will be accomplished with fear and with much suppressed hatred.

Babies from three to six months need, then, to see the mother and to hear her voice at frequent intervals. It is important also that the child take part in the separation which follows, usually by falling asleep. If the mother sits quietly beside the crib or playpen or goes back and forth through the child's room, her presence provides a sense of security while he is falling asleep.

With the growing awareness of himself which comes around six months, moving his own body about, reaching, grasping, sitting up, and putting his hand to his mouth, the baby can tolerate brief periods of being alone. He rapidly learns to make calling sounds, to turn over, to pull himself up and peer in the direction from which his mother usually comes. This approach behavior makes him feel less helpless. He is also ready at this time to form new relationships within the family group, so that the mother can gradually free herself for other activities.

The feelings or emotions of the child at this stage of development have not yet become definitely specialized into forms of expression which we know in the adult as love, hate, and fear; they are in the nature of general body excitement, expressing either well-being or disappointment. We must become accustomed to recognizing the component parts of such a complicated activity as emotion at this early stage of its development. In the beginning of life, the baby reacts automatically, predominantly through the physiological activities—breathing and muscle tone. This somatic component of emotional expression which makes him ready for action is retained in the adult. We find many normal persons who react to strong emotional stimulation in this way, by overeating, smoking, or muscular tension, because the infantile somatic pathways are still called into use.

With these facts in mind, it is startling to discover in discussions with a large group of modern mothers that many of them are not even aware that emotional hunger exists in a baby. Often, in the third month, mothers plan to go back to work without arranging for or accustoming the child to an adequate substitute. This is true of not only the ones who work from necessity but professional women and artists as well. This separation is obviously unsettling to the infant's sense of security. His fundamental breathing, feeling, and eating functions seem well established, but the more subtle and delicate adjustments of his emotional and perceptive life are just beginning. At this time a firm grasp and particularly a basic unfailing relationship with one individual is essential for progressive personality development. As independence is increasing, new persons may be introduced, for fixations occur when a relationship is not shared. This, however, should be gradual with one person at a time and the mother present.

The bugbear of emotional dependency is, like thumb-sucking, a great problem in the mind of many a thoughtful parent. This is one reason why the early development of a strong healthy attachment to the parents is feared and not fostered. It is extremely difficult for parents to appreciate that this first emotional attachment, when understood and directed, is a necessary step in the child's mental development, and it is an important means of educating him. Attempts to temper the child to emotional coldness before he has experienced emotional warmth are much like the old Spartan idea of exposing infants to mobilize courage and fighting strength. This must of necessity take place at the expense of balance in other growth activities.

What, then, about the development of negative emotional reactions when the child experiences repeated frustration of his need for the mother? This leads us to look with a thoughtful and discriminating eye on that well-known nursery cyclone, the temper tantrum. The temper or rage reaction is worthy of close study and should not be dismissed as a mere manifestation of the Devil within. It is based on a very fundamental pattern of behavior: the extensor reaction, previously mentioned as probably the one which brings about birth. Already it has proved useful in the infant's behavior experience as what we might call a very primitive fishlike method of locomotion. Under normal circumstances, this extension or stiffening-out is also part of the development of postural behavior which brings the body into an erect position for standing and walking. The same pattern of behavior we have observed as a response to frustration or disappointment when sucking is interfered with in the early weeks of life—the small torso stiffens out. Obviously, this extension of the body has served to relieve various inner needs. For this reason it comes to have a tremendously important value to the organism of the small child. However, trouble lies in the fact that it readily becomes a main avenue for expressing protest and defensiveness. It is important, therefore, to divert and soothe the child and where possible to avoid the privations which arouse such a response.

Much later on in his development the young child who has been aided will be able to react to disappointment or deprivation psychologically, without the overuse of physiological and motor expression. He can then discharge his excitement either verbally or through appropriate muscular activity. Later he will think out and accept forms of behavior which serve to prevent like disappointments.

To the small child the tantrum is the easiest way of discharging apprehension or anger. The frequent use of this type of behavior before he has become aware of the situation to which he is reacting tends to make it become an automatic activity over which he has great difficulty later in gaining control. Like thumb-sucking and other infantile activities, the tantrum becomes overcharged with functional energy and assumes too much importance in the infantile repertory. Emotional energy undirected may thus become harmful or destructive.

As development continues, two other activities may readily be linked to the early anger reaction—biting and kicking. These important components of eating and locomotion have come into use near the time that emotional reactions become particularly intense. One can see, then, that the first chewing of the infant should be guided toward its physiological purpose. Before the teeth begin to appear, the infant needs to exercise the chewing muscles on hard bread or some suitable food so that the association of chewing and food may be maintained. Puppies, for instance, have violent chewing urges, used on any available object. Before their domestication, biting was an important defense. The impulse to bite is usually strong in babies, also, and the chewing of food has to be encouraged. A breast-fed baby who is vigorous will inevitably bite the breast of the mother, unless he has been generously provided already with some kind of suitable solid food at the time that his teeth begin to appear, which is usually between the fifth and seventh months. Unconsciously the mother is likely to frighten the child through her startle or pain reaction and thus arouse fear in association with chewing. Several mothers in our study group actually slapped the young infants repeatedly for biting the breast, and out of this situation difficult behavior reactions developed which seriously affected the relationship between mother and child. The chewing function itself became inhibited, so that at the age of two years some of these children would chew no solid food.

The same type of inhibition frequently occurs in connection with kicking. Mothers interpret this activity even in the six-months' baby as the expression of bad temper, instead of a preparation for walking. Often when the child is diapered he kicks vigorously, and a nurse or mother who is in a hurry either may attempt to hold the feet forcibly or may gently slap the leg, without realizing the effect of such an unfriendly gesture. This impatient attitude can foster passivity in the child. Obviously, kicking should be freely exercised, since it is an essential part of learning to walk. Aggression is latent in human infants, and nature needs assistance in diverting aggressive energy to the peaceful purposes of muscular growth.

What about early fear reactions in infants? There are two sorts of fear—the innate anxiety which goes with immaturity and helplessness and the fear of dangers outside the body, primarily the loss of the parents. The important connection between these can be made clear. The mechanisms of expressions for both types of feeling are practically the same. The small baby, we might say, fears discomfort of his own inner hungers which he is helpless to satisfy. If they become too intense, they tend to upset his entire physiological equilibrium. His first awareness of discomfort, or unpleasure, as it has been called, is associated with his biological needs—food hunger, inability to breathe well or a feeling of suffocation, and aloneness. His first personal fear is of loss of the mother who supplies these needs which he himself is helpless to satisfy.* Fear develops and becomes intense because his wants are not immediately supplied, and pain and tension arise. The feeling seems to become attached later, automatically, to persons who are not his mother and who do not recognize his needs and to unfamiliar objects in the environment.

Another of the first fears of the infant is fear of the dark. Darkness separates him from his mother and from familiar objects. This illustrates well the relationship between internal and external fear. It seems to be due to two factors: It shuts him off from the mother, whom he cannot see, and it deprives him of a still more primitive satisfaction, one that comes from the stimulation of light. The necessity of seeing, and particularly of seeing the mother, in gaining and maintaining feelings of security is more vitally important than most of us realize. It is the association between the darkness and a corresponding feeling of need that brings about early fear. The child's earliest sense of disturbance, the hunger feeling within himself, may readily become associated with some outside experience, such

---

* See Sigmund Freud, *The Problem of Anxiety* (Albany, Psychoanalytic Quarterly Press, 1936), chap. viii.

as being frightened by loud noises in the dark when his mother is not there to reassure him. Also, pain or discomfort which he experiences externally, like being stuck by a pin or having uncomfortable pressure from his bed coverings, becomes easily associated with the absence of the mother.

We cannot experiment on human babies and give them prescribed experiences of positive or negative emotion, as we experiment with food in order to determine what kind is beneficial and how much can be used, but we can observe the experiments which Nature makes. The unusual case of Baby John shows what may happen when a child is given an unbalanced "diet" of attention. This infant was left motherless at the age of one week in the maternity ward of a large city hospital. The mother, a Spanish refugee temporarily in this country at the time of the war, died suddenly of hemorrhage, and there was no relative to take charge of the small infant. Circumstances in the history of this little waif appealed deeply to the hospital staff, and both nurses and interns developed a remarkable interest in him. They even broke through the rigid formality of nursery rules to give him an unusual amount of personal care. Nurses who had a few minutes off duty would take up the child, hold him, straighten the bed, and otherwise make him comfortable, so that the infant had literally ten mothers instead of one.

For various reasons, the child remained in the hospital three months, so that it was possible to observe closely his early emotional growth. The baby came from humble parentage, and in his ancestry there were no geniuses or college professors, yet his development was head and shoulders above that of any other child studied in either institutions or private homes. Even when he was four weeks old, a visitor coming into the nursery would invariably remark, "That child has personality." There was an alertness and responsiveness in him which was immediately recognizable. At three weeks of age he definitely focused his eyes on the face of the familiar nurse; at five weeks he gave her a fleeting smile of recognition; at two months he held up his head firmly and turned it in response to a call; at three months he made definite cooing sounds and did a great deal of vocalizing.

Obviously, this was not an ideal situation for bringing out the emotional development of the child because so many different people were involved in caring for him, and the effect of closeness to parents was lost; yet because the nurses handling him had undergone careful training and the hospital routine minimized individual variations, he lived under emotional conditions similar to those of an infant with emotionally well-balanced parents.

The sequel to this story is rather distressing. Since no relative claimed the child, he was sent temporarily, at the age of three and a half months, to an institution for homeless children, thereby losing suddenly the abundant, tender, and extremely individualized care which he had been receiving. This institution was an excellent place, and the child suffered no actual neglect of any kind, yet his reaction to the loss of love was dramatic. The first evidence was visible in pallor, the blood apparently receding from the skin, and what the pediatricians call "skin turgor" diminished rapidly. A tendency to sleep a great deal arose, and after a week he developed a mucous diarrhea in spite of a good diet and no evidences of infection. This diarrhea was extremely difficult to control. These physical symptoms brought the child some of the attentions to which he was accustomed, and his physical symptoms improved, but his personality development suffered markedly.

Later it was possible to place John in a carefully selected foster home with a very motherly and understanding woman, to whom the condition was explained. The infant recovered physically, and his body development proceeded at the average rate. The outstanding fact in his subsequent history, however, was his sensitization to any loss of personal attention or love. Separation for one day from the foster mother resulted invariably in an attack of intestinal disturbance, a refusal to eat, or some other physiological manifestation.

It is apparent from observing many infants who, like Baby John, have been deprived of love and from comparing them with others who have flourished under tender personal care, that the ability to love is not a new and independent psychological reaction appearing automatically at a certain period in the child's life and proceeding to develop regardless of outside experiences. It is rather a highly complicated pattern of behavior, beginning physiologically at birth, when the first hungers are appeased, and developing psychologically in response to the presence and care of parents.

Emotion is a part of our equipment for living, and crude outbursts in an infant, whether positive or negative, have a certain survival value for life itself, bringing into action effective behavior which is later appropriated for satisfying still deeper needs. Love, fear, and defense reactions are in time controlled by the intelligence and are put to important uses. "Emotion moves us, hence the word." * It moves us to love, to fight, or to run away—but it can also move us to think.

* See C. S. Sherrington, *The Integrative Action of the Nervous System.* New Haven, Yale University Press, 1906.

12

Getting Ready to Think

WHEN NATURE built the baby she seems to have had a basic plan which could be elaborated in countless ways to meet his needs. Strangely enough, his mind and his digestion have a great deal in common, as we unconsciouly recognize when we use such expressions as "food for thought," "getting the teeth into a problem," "absorbing an idea," or "digesting a book." Both the physical and mental systems get a large part of their initial stimulus to function well from early experience, and just as the first food taken in is a factor in establishing good digestive and assimilative functions, so the routine activities of the baby and the interaction between child and mother contribute in a special way to the development of his awareness and ideation. The infant may have an excellent endowment in the actual protoplasm of his brain yet may never acquire full use of it without stimulus and direction. As we have seen, the first feeling experiences arouse an innate capacity in the brain of the baby to associate inner needs with outer satisfactions. This gives an important impetus to the evolution of mental life.

In discussing the mental status of the baby, therefore, we are concerned with the balanced coordination of all the ac-

tivities of the small organism and particularly with the un-
trammeled vigor with which he learns to satisfy his primal
hungers. Early experiences give him a sense of self. Building up of the metabolism necessary for brain growth and
functioning depends in a peculiar way on these fundamental instinctual drives.

The first evidences of alertness and attention as well as
recognition of persons and objects are in most babies
closely associated with the two dynamic factors, food and
mother; later on father. The ease and pleasure connected
with the satisfaction of the early body needs and with developing emotional hunger or need for love seem to be, to
a large extent, responsible for bringing incentive and direction into the early mental life. Food and parents are the
first realities in the life of a baby, and the cohesion and
stability of his personality are definitely influenced by the
way in which these two essential cravings are satisfied, at
first passively, then actively, through his own seeking. The
kind of intelligence generally considered as abstract thinking is a much later acquisition.

The intensity of the human drives to love and to learn,
as well as their method of expression, are thus closely related to hunger and personal dependency. These drives are
deeply rooted in the helplessness of infancy. The skill and
tenderness of the mother and her actual presence have far-
reaching effects in bringing out the most complete mental
development.

Within the nutritional and breathing systems, nature
has subtly developed the feeling life, the basis of both emo-

tion and thinking, and has related it to muscle action or behavior, which gradually becomes the instrument for mental expression. This is particularly clear with regard to speech. Oral activity, on the one hand, is closely associated with eating and tasting, and, on the other, it is the ultimate expression of both emotions and ideas.

As a result of mothering the child gradually combines and coordinates sucking, or food intake, with sense intake —looking, listening, and grasping—and thus a fairly complicated behavior complex is established. Through these sensory experiences, probably something in the nature of a photographic image is registered in the brain. This mental image, which is the foundation of perception, and the ability to reproduce it through what we know as imagination and memory are the beginning of true mental function. Just as the human embryo is evolved in its characteristic physical form, through constantly absorbing from the mother the necessary chemical elements, so awareness of his own person and of his parents develops in the child's brain in response to the repeated pleasurable experiences coming in over various sense channels connected with body care and organic function. It is considered by some that the first thinking takes place in images or pictures, of which these early sensory experiences are component parts. Recapturing these pictures through memory and adding to them through imagination accomplish an intellectual feat. When the baby has achieved the ability to imagine his mother's presence when she is not there, we may say that his mental functioning is well under way.

For example, when an infant of five or six months hears the familiar door of a nursery open, this signal stimulus seems to call up in his mind a host of associated stimuli (probably in the form of a picture) before the child actually sees the mother. This primitive memory is elicited both by inner need and by outer stimulus. What we can see is a reaction of excitement and well-being, possibly with movements of approach. Concomitant pleasurable sensations of being held, of feeling body warmth, and of being suckled probably begin to develop. This memory does not last long, however, unless an actual mothering experience takes place.

At about the fourth month, the baby's breathing and mouth activity begin to be coordinated in relation to his vocal cords. The sense of touch in the mouth has achieved a new function which is both pleasurable and useful. Parenthetically, it might be mentioned that many women who are charmed with a child's speech avoid his earlier sucking problems as unpleasant, without realizing that speech and intellectual development have a specific relation to sucking. One woman who looked over the manuscript of this book with many comments of agreement and approval hastily skipped the chapter on sucking with the comment, "That wouldn't interest me."

The connection between the two processes is evident, for if we analyze vocalizing we find that the infant does two things: with his tongue he stimulates the hard palate as he did in the first sucking, but at the same time expels his breath, making the two consonant sounds of *da* and *na;*

with his lips he gets an additional lip stimulation with the syllables *ma* and *ba*. Again he uses his breathing and sucking movements in what is the beginning of word formation. As a rule these new vocal activities bring a burst of attention from the mother—an additional source of pleasure to the child, giving him his first feeling of an audience, of having the ability to communicate. He not only hears but is heard. Vocal relationships begin and wordbuilding proceeds rapidly on the basis of these two simple labial and tongue-palate mechanisms. At about the same time, facial expression begins to develop and definite smiling response takes place with the vocalizing. Now he can give as well as take. Soon he will feel like Little Jack Horner, no doubt, "What a big boy am I."

Part of the fun is that muscular coordinations are developing also in the rest of the body. In close connection with the vocalizing, a striving toward the mother, particularly a reaching with the hands and arms, becomes well advanced. The average infant is able to hold his head erect at three months, to look, and to turn his head toward a sound. About two months later the arms have been coordinated with eye, ear, and mouth activity, and the infant whose nervous system is developing smoothly begins to reach, grasp, and to pull himself gradually into a sitting position, and later to crawl. These first motor gropings develop with greater facility when they are definitely directed toward the mother and father.

As response activities make their appearance, the instinctual hungers lose some of their intensity. Energies are diverted into increased awareness and appropriate action. The infant can now maintain for a short time a state of attention, and he shows his first efforts to gratify his own needs. Not only does he want what he wants, but he is going to do something to get it.

This picture of a healthy, happy baby contrasts with the unhappy plight of the child who has been kept emotionally detached from his parents to avoid the danger of exaggerated dependency. Such a deprived child is already inadequately equipped for life. His appetites and longings have been frustrated, and he has little impulse to love. In consequence, there is an imbalance between physiological coordination and emotional behavior. Not only do irregularities of breathing appear but vocalization also tends to be disturbed, and there is with some infants a tendency toward croup and asthma. Such babies may also have a chronically poor appetite, along with either constipation or diarrhea, or else they are overweight. As a rule, they are either hyperactive, as far as general body movement goes, and inclined to be extremely distractable or are preoccupied with some sort of repetitious activity. They center on themselves the attention that would normally go out to the parents. They have difficulty in focusing either their organic reactions or their general body movements. For example, such a baby of six months, when given his bottle does not reach and vocalize; when the bottle is put in his mouth, he does not respond with steady holding and firm sucking, followed by satisfied relaxation. On the contrary, he is rather indifferent to the bottle, looks here and there, moves about restlessly, and interrupts his sucking at frequent intervals. His hunger sense has become diffuse, and the activities associated with food-getting are not well knit together. Pleasure and comfort, necessary to cement these acts, are lacking. Security in the relationship to the mother (or her consistent substitute) is the basis for good eating and eliminating behavior as well as for the start of smooth mental development and educability.

Infants who do not have a definite and direct emotional attachment to the mother show various forms of distorted behavior, either in their eating and elimination or in their speech or locomotion. They may be precocious in speaking and very slow in learning to walk, or vice versa. Later on in life, these children have great difficulty in building up their first relationships with other members of the family group and thus are unable to find the emotional outlet which they so urgently need. They may later on develop brilliant abilities in certain limited fields, but are inclined to show early disturbances of personality and are incapable of establishing good personal relationships.

An interesting piece of information, bearing directly on the subject of the linking of emotional with intellectual development, was recently communicated to the writer by Margaret Mead, who has made intensive study of parental care among the natives of Bali and Samoa. Infants in these islands have complete liberty as far as sucking is concerned, and their first instinctual needs in this respect are fairly well taken care of. However, their emotional ties are never soundly built up. These babies are cared for by any member of the family, including the father, grandmother, and small brothers and sisters, and apparently the emotions get no initial focus on the parents. They may even suckle from a number of different women. They are purposely made to feel jealous, and any close attachment to the mother is ridiculed. The result seems to be that emotional and social relationships throughout life remain insecure, for they are based chiefly on food satisfaction and protection against strangers outside the group. It is not surprising to find that the sex drive of these children is precocious, since no attempt is made to sublimate it through the medium of a good parental leadership, which it tends to replace. The emotional integration and intellectual development which civilized children can reach before school age is not fostered. Intellectually, these children are not defective, and some of them have been educated along certain lines with success, even in such abstract training as mathematics, through the personal effort of a teacher to whom the child has become attached. However, when taken out of the familiar environment of the group, these children cannot maintain independence and self-control, and either they go into a deep depression which cripples them so that they cannot function or else they sicken and die.

Certain striking general correlations become evident in studying the developmental sequence of behavior in a large number of babies with close regard to the type of parental care that they have received. For those children whose parents are more nearly mature emotionally and who have consistently made good personal adjustments in life, mental development proceeds much more rapidly and is definitely better integrated. Such parents do not make use of the child as a necessary companion or as a play object, but they recognize intuitively and respect, usually through definite study, the essential nature and actual personal needs of the infant; they are not obsessed with fear either that the child may become too much attached to them or that his mentality is somehow inadequate or his erotic expression precocious; and, if some temporary anomaly arises, they are not fearful of calling for expert advice.

On the other hand, it is interesting to note, from the close month-to-month development of babies whose mothers are emotionally detached or absorbed in social, professional, or artistic pursuits, that retardation is evident in speech or locomotion or that dissociated activities which we know as habits have appeared. There is manifest unhappiness. Such babies invariably have eating problems and disturbances of elimination; they sleep too little and tend to be hyperactive and not well organized, or they may have developed, already, an exaggerated tendency to auto-erotic practices.

Testing of "intelligence" in a child under a year of age is a questionable procedure. Unless there has been some obvious brain damage, the only factors which can be estimated with any degree of accuracy, without a continuous day-by-day observation over a period of at least a week, are the general eating adequacy, the ability to focus emotionally, and the nature of vocalizing. Perhaps the most significant factor in the mental life at this time is the stability of the child's physiological activity, his ability to maintain motor coordination and to sleep under the stress of slight changes of routine or temporary withdrawal of the mother. A poorly integrated infant will react to any changes with organic disorders rather than with some immediate, psychological protest. The better integrated child will react with crying or with hyperactivity, perhaps in the nature of looking for what he has lost. He becomes demanding.

A simple test is suggested which may prove useful for determining the stability of babies between six and twelve months of age whose early development has not already been closely observed. This test must be conducted in the child's own room, and he must not become aware of a strange observer's presence. Such a test is valid only if detailed information has been obtained and it is known that the child's routine experiences in the previous twenty-four hours have been the usual ones. The test, of course, would not apply where disturbing incidents have preceded it.

Integration test. As the child is waking from a nap, and just before any of his routine feedings (preferably in the afternoon), his mother comes into the room to nurse him and sits beside the crib; or, his bottle containing milk is placed by his mother or familiar nurse on a small table in full view of the crib. The bottle is immersed in hot water for warming.

I. Well-integrated babies between six and twelve months of age give the following reactions: Attention is focused alternately on the bottle and the mother (food hunger and emotional need are becoming differentiated); there is immediately some motor reaction, indicating pleasurable excitement in the younger baby—kicking, arm waving, and vocalizing, with a general tendency to reach toward the mother. The older child will pull himself up to a standing position or else crawl toward the mother. These reactions indicate good mental response.

II. The child who is less well integrated, who has been allowed to remain hungry or too much alone, or who has suffered from illness or accidents, reacts with diffuse restlessness and crying, but makes litttle coordinated response when he sees either his mother or the bottle. Such a child is living under constant tension. His hungers either develop to such a degree when food or mother appears that they overpower him (he becomes frantic and cries) or else they have become diffuse, and any organized reaction, such as vocalizing or striving toward the mother, is precluded.

III. The baby who has suffered from persistent frustration, either instinctual or emotional, shows a definitely pathological reaction. This type of child, after a fleeting recognition of the food-mother situation, shows little further attention. As a rule, he becomes distracted immediately by some other interest or else may fall asleep again, making no coordinated attempt to reach for what he needs. This type of reaction has a sinister implication for both physical and mental health and means that the child's initial ability to recognize and cope with basic needs has become disorganized. Efforts toward reorganization should be begun promptly.

Type I child has a nominal degree of security and coordination, due to consistent satisfaction of instinctual and emotional hungers. In consequence, he has reached a higher level of mental development. The faculty of attention is sustained for an appreciable length of time. Clear recognition, pleasure reaction and anticipation to both food and mother, and some degree of appropriate response are all evident. Instead of immediately crying, attempts at communication (speech) are made.

Type II child, who cries immediately, is reacting on an anxiety basis. He is so insecure that he is immediately overcome either by fear of disappointment or by rage, and his energy is dissipated negatively.

Type III child has already set up protective reactions (indifference) against those hungers which are fundamental in his development.

It becomes evident, then, that the linking of various levels of mental and premental life takes place in a subtle and often in an entirely unrecognized fashion and that the most important element in facilitating this interassociation of various levels of mental life is consistent parental care.

13

Toward Mental Health

WE ARE generally agreed that humans are one of Nature's most successful experiments. There were many ways of providing for the care of the young before Nature tried her hand at mammals. Previously one of the successful steps in evolution was the egg-laying species. Sometimes this method involved care of the young after the eggs were hatched, and sometimes, as in the case of the cold-blooded reptiles like the dinosaur, the female laid the eggs in the sand, the sun did the hatching, and the infants were left in the hands of fate. There are some modern parents who seem to think this was a good idea; they do not wish to be "burdened" with the care of an infant. With regard to breast-feeding, mothers say with spirit that they are not going to be cows. They seem even to prefer to be dinosaurs.

When scientists found unhatched dinosaur eggs in the sand near some of the bones of the dinosaur parents, they speculated on what went wrong with the system. After careful study, we can safely assume that one cause of their extinction was lack of protection of their young.

Undoubtedly an important factor in man's ascendancy to his supreme position is the consistent care and love of the parents through the long period of helpless infancy. If in times of war we wonder whether something has gone wrong with our present system, we may perhaps find one answer in our still inadequate understanding of the instinct of aggression in human nature and of the way it may be aroused by frustration and friction in early relationships. If human nature is to reach a higher potential of development, if anxiety and unhappiness are to be lessened in small children, the emotional needs of infants will have to be recognized and appeased from the beginning.

In the preceding pages the attempt has been made to clarify the significance to the infant of a warm relatedness to his parents. This subtle tie which originates through providing need satisfaction and comfort is a vital stimulus to the child's psychological growth and later emotional maturing. As we have seen, it primes into action certain vital reflexes, it arouses sensory awareness and gradually provides a life-giving sense of functional security. In time it helps to promote awareness of a separate maturing self with a readiness to participate and adapt to the family environment.

When parents are preoccupied or lack warmth and understanding, the lonely and vigorous infant will activate and solace himself with thumb-sucking, body rolling, and other repetitive activities which may become the basis for undesirable "habits," or else he may withdraw into listlessness and sleep, later into exaggerated daydreaming. When vigorous "training" and discipline are begun before a good relationship is established and the child senses that life is good, automatic resistance mechanisms are aroused. He may cry persistently, not sleep well or eat well, and may even become resentful to personal approach.

The guiding of this relationship toward a complete maturing of the child's potentialities and to later self-dependence requires on the part of parents wisdom, self-discipline, love, and a deep understanding of child nature and needs. Mismanagement is illustrated in the two following studies of young adults, in whom early traumatic experiences were influential factors in producing exaggerated anxiety states and inappropriate defenses which eventually lead to pathological depression and dependency on alcohol.

Sue, a young girl in her early twenties, was brought by her mother to the writer for psychiatric help because of serious alcoholism and because her premature marriage had gone completely on the rocks. Her history showed from the statements of her mother that she had not been a wanted child. Both parents had been looking forward to the birth of a boy (the first child was a girl, three years older). Nevertheless, because it was a family custom, the mother planned to breast-feed her, and the first three months were passed without obvious difficulty. Then the mother contracted pneumonia and was severely ill for several weeks, so that the child had to be abruptly weaned. She lost both mother and food. She was put in the care of a practical nurse, a warm and motherly woman, who remained in the family for three years. The effect of the sudden change was not apparent at the time.

According to the mother, she was greatly relieved to be freed from the care of the baby girl and left her entirely in the charge of the nurse (who was a devoted and indulgent woman). Another child was born to this mother (a baby boy) when Sue was two years old. The mother lavished her entire affection upon the little brother, and there was scarcely any relationship between herself and Sue, who turned completely to the kindly foster mother. At the age of two and one-half a dramatic incident took place, which showed something of the child's feelings. Sue took her mother's wedding ring, which had been accidentally left in the bathroom, and hid it, in order to give it as a present to her nurse. The mother, whose marriage was an unstable one, became panicky over the loss of the ring, and accused the nurse of stealing it. Sue was frightened at her mother's agitation, but secretly gave the ring to the nurse, with the remark, "You are my mama." The nurse, in turn, became alarmed because of the mother's accusations and dropped the ring into the toilet, where it was discovered later by a plumber.

From this time on, the mother's suspicions increased. She was secretly jealous of the woman who had been so successful with her little daughter. At the end of the third year, the nurse was abruptly dismissed. Sue was left in an anxious and distressed state, not understanding at all what had happened. She was put in the care of a housemaid and her own sister, who was only three years older. Evidently, at this time severe separation anxiety developed in the child along with a deep antagonism toward her mother and baby brother. She became a serious behavior problem, restless, defiant of her parents, untidy, often refusing to eat. As the mother expressed it, "Sue became completely unmanageable" at this time. (She had been trained without difficulty by the nurse.) Between the two sisters a strong and somewhat unhealthy relationship gradually grew with exaggerated erotic play. Both of them resented the baby brother and the attention given to him by the mother.

Sue was eager to enter kindergarten and made consistently good grades in school, and it was for the most part at home that her behavior was incorrigible. The older sister went to college when Sue was fourteen, and this separation again increased her erratic behavior at home.

At the age of seventeen Sue was ready to enter college, where her sister was now a junior. She was again to be rejected. Much preoccupied with her own interests and with new friends, the older sister paid her very little attention. Sue was deeply crushed by this indifference. She did not make friends, but became introspective and extremely aggressive toward her sister. Before the end of her first year in college it was discovered that she was stealing various objects, costly perfume and jewelry and small amounts of money from other students. She had no need for these things that she took, but seemed to be reaching out blindly for something that was lacking in her emotional life, much as she had reached for the ring in her need to secure a mother when she was a small child. She was abruptly expelled from college for stealing. This brought deep disgrace on herself, her sister, and her parents.

Following this experience, Sue began for the first time to take a lively interest in men (she had hated her brother and scarcely knew her father). For a year she became quite promiscuous and overindulged in drinking. This naturally brought increasing distress to her parents, who now had no control over her. They branded her as an eccentric and degenerate girl.

In desperation, Sue became engaged at nineteen to a wealthy bachelor much older than herself, obviously a parent figure, and they were married the following year when she was twenty, much to the relief of her family, who felt that she had at last been saved. As would be expected, the marriage was not a success. Sue's husband began to take long "business trips" to avoid the arguments, her flirtations, and other deviant behavior, such as constant extravagance, especially in ordering expensive jewelry.

Not long before coming for therapy, Sue had become fast friends with a neighbor, a married woman whose husband was also away a great deal. They drank heavily together, and within a few months, both had become quite dependent on each other and on large quantities of alcohol. The friend, it was discovered, was ill with a breast cancer, for which she had to be operated. She died under the operation, and the effect of this last separation was too much for Sue. She became deeply depressed, and her drinking became so excessive that her parents brought her for psychiatric help.

Jack was the first child of young college-trained parents who had found serious problems in their marriage relationship. When Jack was born, his mother lavished on him an excess of the love that rightfully belonged to her husband, who in turn plunged intensively into a number of active business ventures and was away from home a great deal. The little boy was breast-fed for eighteen months, and no other food was introduced. (His mother liked to nurse him.) She fondled him to excess, constantly hovering over him and attempting to supply every need before the child himself experienced it. He slept at his mother's side or in her bed. She unfortunately did not look ahead to his need for self-development and even at a year did not consider the beginnings of the child's independence. This relationship was actually a miniature love affair. Finally, on the occasion of a minor illness the pediatrician came into the picture and insisted that it would be necessary to introduce the child to other foods else he would become anemic. The mother took this literally and attempted to wean him from the breast abruptly. The child refused to drink from a glass and rejected each food that was offered him. Tension grew. At this time the father stepped in and attempted to feed the little boy. He took him away from his mother and with every inducement tried to coax him to eat other foods and to drink milk from a glass. For two days the child took nothing except small sips of water and became extremely anxious and listless. His mother was in a similar state and became so nervous that she paced the floor constantly. In great alarm the pediatrician was again called in (he was a genial country doctor). He took the child into the kitchen, petted and played with him and finally was able to induce him to drink a small quantity of milk. His fast was finally broken, and little by little the father taking over the entire care of the child was able to induce him to eat. Jack became a dreamer, passive and unable to play. When he was three years old, a sister was born, and he interpreted the newcomer to mean that his mother no longer wanted him. He began to wander away whenever he was left by himself and was often found at the home of a neighbor. This running away became so exaggerated that the child had to be kept in his own back yard by means of a rider on the clothesline. (This was the first and most vivid memory of his childhood.)

At the age of five he was put in kindergarten, the parents hoping that he would learn to play with other children under good care. He seemed relieved to be away from home and gradually made a fairly good adjustment, as he did later in school life, but his behavior at home became quite passive and without initiative.

Jack was a child of unusual intelligence and got a scholarship to a fine university. There he developed an exaggerated attachment to his roommate, a boy his own age. The two young men began drinking together and repeatedly got into trouble by aggressive acts in the community. The friend withdrew from the university, and Jack went into a deep depression because of this loss. He began drinking more heavily and had to be placed in a sanitarium for treatment because of depression with suicidal attempts.

How may we interpret in the illness of these two young people some of the lasting effects due to traumatic emotional conditions in early life? From information coming to light during a long course of therapy, as well as from the history given by parents, the sequence of disturbing events and the characteristic defense reactions of each of the two became clear. Both were without the necessary father influence from the start. The young woman with the impression of having lost friendly emotional support from her mother tended to grasp for a new person (or thing) who seemed to offer security. Through repeated disappointments, her anxieties and tension became apparent in childhood in aggressive defiant behavior, jealousy of her younger brother, and an erotic attachment to her sister. Later in college she reacted to failure in relationships by petty stealing of jewelry and perfume which led to her expulsion as an erratic and dishonest individual. A number of immature relationships with inappropriate "dates" together with exaggerated indulgence in alcohol to numb her sense of failure led to a marriage which was spoiled by the inevitable continuation of unstable aggressive activity, extravagance, and flirtations. Finally, in a dependent, possessive friendship with another woman, she lost out again and reacted with a severe depression.

What had happened to Jack at eighteen months in spite

of the fact that his physical health was good and he could walk and talk? He had failed to develop awareness of his own identity and had no initiative. He could not eat, sleep, or eliminate except in his mother's or father's presence. His feeling of an independent self was wanting. If left alone to play with toys for a few minutes, he panicked and cried for his mother. Feelings of infantile helplessness persisted into later life as a crippling passivity.

With the birth of his sister and the daily observation of the new baby receiving the constant love and care of his mother, an overwhelming jealousy was aroused. From the tension of this jealousy he took bodily flight and later became a daydreamer. Though he was intelligent, he did well in school because his father saw to it that learning was poured into him by especially devoted teachers. In adolescence he became somewhat feminine, was obsessed by fantasies of himself as a mother tenderly caring for a younger boy. Led into drinking during high school, he came to rely on this artificial form of stimulation to numb his apprehension about dates with girls. Finally in college, his roommate, who could not stand the highly possessive relationship between them, withdrew from college. This precipitated Jack into a suicidal depression.

Emotionally crippled young people such as these two are seen frequently by psychiatrists, but often too late to remedy satisfactorily the personality distortion which has taken place. It becomes increasingly evident that most of the emotional problems of children and adolescents begin with traumatic relational situations in early life. Like marasmus, rickets, and other physical diseases of infancy these mental distortions must be understood and prevented. Modern parents need to acquaint themselves with the facts of mental as well as physical development.

It may seem to the modern woman that this picture of the early mother-child relationship neglects the rights of the mother, who is an individual with outside interests of her own. The madonna has been painted mostly by male artists who saw the ideal woman completely—and permanently—dedicated to a child. Today many women are as deeply and successfully involved in business or professional duties as are men. Yet both can be adequate parents if they put thought, understanding, and planning to work. Perhaps with new psychological insight into the dynamics of a child's mental growth, the meaning of motherhood and fatherhood may assume its rightful dignity, interest, and joy, and the temporary withdrawal from a career for a woman in order to create and nurture a new life may not be regarded as demeaning or as an unwanted interruption or sacrifice. Association with womanly women who have enjoyed the experience of childbirth and infant rearing will often help a young expectant mother to relinquish any artificial attitudes and to get the unique mental stimulus which comes from contact with first principles of life. If there is such a thing as a "touchstone of truth" for a woman, it is likely to be found in the experience of childbearing and of psychological mothering. That her husband is capable and interested in assuming his father role from the start in this joint adventure assures a more successful outcome.

The period covered by this small book is that segment of growth and maturing which is usually called infancy. But we dare not overlook the fact that in these first two years are the infant's first schooling in the fundamentals of life, attaining liberty, and the pursuit of happiness. First reaction experiences in learning to live and love persist because they are related to survival. Life is a continuous developing process and a look into the child's future may help in directing the present just as a glance into the past helped to explain many factors in the newborn. The most intense conflict arising somewhat later in the child's life as a result of inadequate or inconsistent parental concern and bringing him uneasiness and guilt feelings and parents' deep disapproval is that of precocious sex habits. A lonely child turns to himself for solace. Under ideal conditions in which the parents are emotionally healthy and the baby is wanted and loved, erotic impulses do not necessarily become a problem in the first years, though they are definitely in evidence. However, this ideal condition is rare. When the emotional needs of the child are unsatisfied or when the relationship with one parent is overdeveloped because of insecurity in marriage, sex habits tend to become exaggerated. The unmothered infant if he is vigorous and robust will stimulate himself with various kinds of rhythmical body activities if normal fondling and rocking are denied him. This self-stimulation is often the beginning of excessive childhood masturbation since it leads inevitably to stimulation of the genital organs. In turn, this premature and excessive stimulation brings about general uneasiness in the child and arouses disapproval and anxiety in parents. A conflict of great dynamic intensity is thus established between the child and his environment which may last throughout life.

From the physiological point of view as well as from the emotional this premature exaggeration of the child's erotic impulses is unfortunate. Nature has muted the sex urge in human babies, but when it has been aroused it cannot be summarily suppressed. Prevention of this condition by maintaining warm family ties with the child and by the early provision for the natural expression of his pleasure needs in play is the surest remedy. It is a serious task to attempt to divert sexual energy into new channels of interest once it is established, and it is only by considering the early rights of infants that we can forestall those wrongs which later on the family or society feels obliged to deal with harshly.

Thus, as we have seen, poor relationship with the parents leads to the establishing of protest reactions on both sides which tend to become the basis of adult personality disorders. The most important asset of a baby as he begins life is two emotionally healthy parents. His deepest need is the understanding and consistent care of his parents. We must recognize the dangerous implications of unhappiness and emotional instability in the young child and understand that emotional disturbance in the parents is as infectious to an infant as is tuberculosis or syphilis. If this sounds shocking to the reader, let each take it to heart and act.

Those parents who shrink in revulsion from the primitive developmental side of a child's life make it impossible for him to mature with the very qualities of intelligence and self-reliance and honesty that they think they stand for. If they are to be worthy parents of a contented infant, groping his way upward like any living thing, they will have to cultivate a new form of fastidiousness founded on knowledge of biological and psychological reality. There is no other way to guide the baby toward mental health.

Index